# BODY BLISS

THE JOURNEY TO
*body acceptance*

BODY BLISS
The Journey to Body Acceptance



Cover Design - Michelle Fairbanks
Editing - Megan Jackson and Donna Zuniga
Interior Design - Michelle Fairbanks

ISBN Print - 978-1-990352-30-0

For more information, visit leadherpublishing.com
instagram.com/leadherpublishing

For more information on the Lead Author, visit balancebliss.blog
instagram.com/balanceblissblog

# BODY BLISS

## THE JOURNEY TO *body acceptance*

ANDREA MONDOUX | COURTNEY ST. CROIX

ALICIA THURSTON . AMANDA CASE . AMIE MARIANA SIDER
ANGELA PHILLIPS . BRITTANY SCHMIDT . ERIN ELLA ZARZECZNY
FRAN R GARTON . JENNIFER HEARD . JILLIAN GRANT
JOANNA MENEZES . LYN HOUSSER . NICOLE JACKSON
NIOMI MENDLER . SARAH CONNORS . VICKY JOMAA

# Contents

# *Introduction*

## ANDREA MONDOUX

AUTHOR PHOTO: ALICIA THURSTON PHOTOGRAPHY
balancebliss.blog | IG: @balanceblissblog

I know what you might be thinking… is this another book about your body? Another book about how women come in all different shapes and sizes and that is what makes us beautiful?

YES, it is!

Books like this are still very much needed because no matter where we are on our journey, it is a conscious and continuous process to reframe the way we think. The process of healing the years of negative self-talk and harmful things we have done to ourselves to look and feel a certain way is a long one. Society has spent decades conditioning us to feel negatively about our bodies. It is so deeply rooted in our culture that sometimes we aren't even aware of our subconscious biases around our bodies, our worthiness, and our beauty. You're not alone in your thoughts.

Thanks a lot, diet culture!

When I say, "diet culture," I mean the massive industry that profits from making most women feel, in some way, unworthy – like we need to be a certain way, fit into a certain size, or meet a certain expectation. And if we don't, then it makes us feel like we need to be doing something to achieve that criteria.

Too small, too big.
Too wide, too narrow.
Too flat, too lumpy.
Too masculine, too feminine…
Not enough.

The sales pitches and messaging are relentless. There is this idea that there is only one body type, and it is the one that we should strive to achieve. If we physically represent anything outside that mould, it festers feelings of shame and unworthiness.

Here's something that you maybe didn't know: For the frequency at which people choose to participate in a diet, over 95% of diets fail. Read that again: 95%. And yet, the diet industry is booming despite being the ONLY industry with the largest and most consistent failure rate globally. I think it's safe to say that any other industry, product, or service wouldn't be as lucrative or survive with these metrics. So what's going on?!

Humans crave connection and belonging. We want to fit in and be a part of something; it's in our nature. And when you combine this desire for belonging with the standards we're told that we need to achieve to fit in, it's a recipe for disaster. We start to look outside ourselves to fit in, and then we fall victim to these standards and desire for acceptance. We begin to believe that we need to meet these standards – to get the job, to be seen as successful, and desirable – and too often, it's an endless need to define our value or be acknowledged.

This brainwashing and conditioning comes in different forms (it's everywhere): billboards, commercials, magazines, and movie screens. Day in and day out, whether they be one-off comments or things that we hear every day, the words of strangers or even the people we love, it's always coming at us. Consistent messaging plays on our insecurities, which we subconsciously internalize, and soon it becomes our inner dialogue. Our brains are very impressionable – we are all susceptible to it – and when we are continuously exposed to something, we start to believe it. The thing is, women have been exposed to this self-deprecating dialogue for too long, and the jig is up! It's time to reframe our thinking, create new conversations, and reset our inner dialogue. If we can be influenced into believing one thing, then let's rewrite the story and create our beliefs.

That's why we created this book.

We need another book to continue to reset and re-frame our thinking – to remind us of our value and to accept our body where it is, right now! We need to let go of worthiness coming when you achieve x, y, and z. We need to undo the way that society has programmed us – to not feel so alone.

This book does not claim to teach you to feel massive self-love, though, because sometimes that is a big ask. You will start to see that even as these women wrote their chapters, they were and are still working through these stories and beliefs. This book is here to help YOU, the average, everyday woman, to let go of perfection and learn through the stories of other women just like you. Together we will learn to give ourselves some grace and to start or continue the journey to body acceptance.

As a Holistic Health Coach, Bestselling Author and self-proclaimed Empower-er of Women, at the heart of what I do with my clients is a deep empathy and reflection phase about what I would have needed when I was in my darkest moments. In case you are wondering, here are what some of my darkest moments looked like

- There were days that I could barely look at myself in the mirror.
- I didn't want to get dressed or leave the house because I thought nothing looked good on my body.
- Some days I was in tears, ashamed of my body.
- I felt so alone.

What did I need in those moments? What could I read for inspiration? Who did I need to hear from or connect with that could help me find hope and confidence to make me believe that I had value?

It was then that the answer seemed pretty simple. I needed to hear from other women – all types of women, just like me and different from me, from all walks of life – validating my thoughts and showing me that I was not alone. I was not alone in my struggle, and someday, somehow, I was going to be able to move past it. I needed to hear that things weren't going to be this dark forever because they had been there too, and had come out on the other side.

Those days are never far from my mind, and in fact, as I write this introduction, I have reached a valley in my acceptance journey – but I KNOW the value of sharing stories. Sharing stories is the strength, experience, and empathy that I bring to my practice and how I lead women, inspiring them in their journey – and this is exactly where my heart is with this book.

## HERE ARE SOME STATS FOR THE ANALYTICAL WOMEN OUT THERE:

**5** – The age that little girls don't care about how the clothes they wear make their bodies look. They open the closet in the morning and wear whatever jumps out at them (sometimes multiple outfits per day). They wear what they wear simply because it makes them happy and feel good.

**11** – The average age that girls start puberty, cueing all of the body changes that are different for everyone. You know what I am talking about. Hips may get a little wider, shirts start to get a little tighter. They start to become acutely aware of other female bodies around them and they are influenced by how female bodies are portrayed in the media.

**13** – The average age when girls begin to develop body image issues. Research has shown that around 50% of American girls reported being unhappy with their bodies. Most alarming is that in just 4 years, this skyrockets to 80% by the time they reach 17.

Sounds about right on time, according to my experience.

I remember the picture from an end of year grade eight pool party with five of my best friends. I was 13 or 14. I had bought my first two-piece bathing suit and this was a big deal for me. I wasn't comfortable in my body but I knew that the other girls would be wearing 2-pieces and I wanted to fit in. It was lime green and I had opted for the boy shorts style as I was not feeling confident enough for a bikini style bottom. I still remember strategically placing my arm over my stomach in the group picture on the diving board, embarrassed because my stomach was too big and my hips felt too wide. It makes me sad now to think back to my 13-year-old self, that at this age, these were my self-deprecating thoughts about my body.

It's easy to look back now with confidence and the knowledge that the internal dialogue and thoughts were simply a result of what I was exposed to in society and what I envisioned was the standard of beauty, but it was still so challenging to be in it. And I would wager maybe you have had a similar experience.

Truth be told, I have had countless experiences like this since then. I am often hyper-aware that I was and always have been the bigger girl, feeling

YOUR *beautiful* LIFE
WILL CYCLE IN AND
OUT OF SEASONS; SOME
YOU'LL ENJOY MORE
THAN OTHERS, BUT EACH
DAY IS A NEW DAY.

ashamed of my body because I couldn't shop at the same stores that my skinny friends shopped at. When I shopped with them, I always bought the biggest size (which was 13 at the time) and sometimes it wouldn't even fit me right. I struggled to feel comfortable in them. Let's never bring back low-rise jeans, okay?

I never felt attractive around boys. I felt like I was not pretty by what society deemed as beautiful and desirable to a boy. It was always on my mind. I felt it in the way people looked at me, the attention I didn't get (and craved), and it was obvious in the way people interacted with me (or didn't).

There is still much ingrained in us about what women should look like and I am thankful to see that there has been some progress in body representation and casting in the media, but man do we EVER have a ways to go.

In my body acceptance journey over the last seven years, I have come to realize those ideals that exist on the outside will always continue to exist in some way; there will be no way to completely eradicate them. But I've also realized that a lot of my experiences were perpetuated by the way I felt about myself – because I let them. They were amplified by the way that I talked to myself, the way that I looked at myself, and the way that I measured my worth (which was not a lot, because I didn't look like "that"). And I realized that if things were really going to change for me, I needed to change the way that I viewed myself, the way that I talked to myself, and most importantly the way that I took care of and valued myself, beyond simply what my body looked like. I have realized that my weight and my size are the least important things about me. I now know that my size 18 jeans and my 5' 10" height have no direct correlation to how successful, valuable, and important my role in this world is.

## SO WHAT ELSE HAVE I LEARNED ALONG THE WAY?

I've learned that most people around you don't care nearly as much about your body as you think they do.

I've also learned that no matter how far you've come, there will always be days when you feel a bit off in your own skin – that's part of your journey, part of life. **Your beautiful life will cycle in and out of seasons; some you'll enjoy more than others, but each day is a new day.** It doesn't mean that you need to seek out the quickest diet or fastest way to lose weight, or that you shouldn't eat that day; maybe today is just a leggings and baggy sweater kind of day instead. The skinny jeans can wait until tomorrow.

You can wear whatever you want! Whatever makes you feel comfortable! Remember, NO one has the right to tell you otherwise. Your body is yours and yours only, and it should be celebrated with clothing. Buy clothes to fit your unique and beautiful body as it is right now. Don't hold onto things that don't fit, hoping they will one day. Relieve yourself of the pressure; it doesn't serve you. Find something that fits right. Clothes were meant to fit our bodies; bodies were not meant to change to fit into clothes. Now say that one again before you move on.

It's okay to want to change your body, and you can also accept it at the same time. These two feelings can co-exist. It doesn't have to be one or the other. I, too, fell into the self-love, body positivity trap, thinking that to be in the "right place" and to have it how I was taught to have it, I needed to love every part of my body. That never resonated with me. I didn't feel that way– so I felt wrong.

*"Do I have to love every single part of my body?"* (No!)

I've realized that you don't have to love everything about your body, and just because you don't doesn't mean you have to hate it, either – you can simply accept it!

You can accept your body and want to take better care of it through movement, boundaries, and nutrition. You can accept your body and still want to release some weight. Weight loss isn't a bad thing; it just becomes a slippery slope when you're tying it to your worth and your happiness. Accepting it simply means giving it compassion and living in the hate of it. Anything done from a place of hate has negative energy around it. Bring more positivity into your life.

*Loving yourself is OKAY.*

*Doing things to support your body and take care of it from a place of love is OKAY.*

*Being confident is OKAY!*

You don't need to compare yourself to anyone else. You are different from them, and you don't need to be like anyone else. You are enough!

Lastly, no one has the answers to who you are at your core – only your soul and your intuition know that. Listen to it, honor it, and trust it. Protect yourself from negative influences and negative people. If you are feeling vulnerable, stay away from negativity, and for the love of all things holy, stay off the internet!

Grab this book, read through all the unique, life-changing stories of women who are just like you and me, and remember that you are NEVER alone, babe!

And if you ever need anything, I am always here to listen, share a motivational message, and inspire you to be your best self. Never hesitate to reach out.

# Chapter 1

## ALICIA THURSTON

AUTHOR PHOTO: LAUREL LEAF PHOTOGRAPHY
Aliciathurston.com | IG: @aliciathurstonphotography

I can't ever remember a time when I felt fully comfortable and at home in my body. Even at the age of six, I had a thought that no one would ever be inside my head, see with my eyes, no one would ever fully understand what it's like to be me – and it was an incredibly lonely and isolating feeling. It wasn't until I was 39 that I started to feel some sense of body acceptance.

After 10 years of marriage, two kids, many moves, lots of travel, and running a successful photography business for over a decade, none of it made me feel worthy of taking up space in my body. There was always an internal memo that read, "*When I lose weight*, I can wear the clothes, be outgoing, be myself, take up space in this world, be valued, I'll do _______!"

I had done all of the things, and checked all of the things off my list that I knew I wanted to accomplish by the time I turned 40, except for this one big thing that I didn't even realize was on my list: BODY ACCEPTANCE!

Until I was 39, and my second child went off to kindergarten, I had plenty to keep me busy and preoccupied with taking care of everything else but myself. Then suddenly, I was alone during the day and had time to myself, and I saw that I had to take ownership and start to do the work. That was a hard thing, but I was ready.

So here I am at 42, and writing this chapter has me coming face-to-face with how much more work I have to do. I feel like I have only just tapped the surface. But that's the thing – the work is never really over. I once heard the phrase, "If you're not growing, you're dying." So who doesn't want to be growing? Sign me up, even if it's hard AF!

Let's go back to where the problem started: it's not pretty, and I'll put in a trigger warning here for anyone who can't read about eating disorders or sexual violence. Stop here if that's you.

I had so many unhealthy messages growing up.

I was four years old when my parents split, and my mom got a nanny when we moved to Toronto because she was a full-time executive in the corporate world. My nanny was wonderful and loving and years later she told me that I cried all the time after the separation and her heart ached for me, so she would give me a chocolate bar to take my mind off the hurt. Enter my eating disorder. Eating my emotions was a learned way to deal with the hard things.

When I brought up this story during a Brené Brown "Daring Way" workshop that I took a few years ago, another participant asked if I was angry with my nanny for her way of managing my pain. My response was: "No, I can't be. She did the best that she could with the tools that she had at the time."

As I grew out of my baby-ish body, I can only assume that's when it started to become unacceptable to some that I wasn't a skinny kid.

"If you keep eating ice cream you'll end up like that!" Pointing to a fat woman crossing the street. Internal message: you shouldn't eat something because you'll get fat. Fat is bad. I am bad.

"You don't need another piece of cake!" Internal message: I don't know how to make my own choices, and I can't be trusted to know when enough is enough.

"Haha, do you stuff your bra!?!" Being teased by the boys in grade 6 was a regular thing. Internal message: my body is not normal AND people have an opinion about it.

"You look great, have you lost weight?" Said by so many people throughout my life. Internal message: people place value on my body, and comment positively only when it gets smaller. The smaller the better.

"If you took your face and put it on her (my best friend) body, you would have the perfect woman." My high school boyfriend felt the need to share that with me. Internal message: well, I think that one's pretty clearly damaging and fucked up.

All of these messages were from the people who "loved" me. I don't believe any of them were ill intentioned, but they were all damaging. Add in the medical professionals who always looked at my weight as a cause and a problem, the magazines and media we were bombarded with in the 80s and 90s with the "heroin chic" look, and it's no wonder why so many people suffer from a skewed perspective of beauty.

Having a sweet tooth became part of my identity; it still is, if I'm being honest. I remember feeling embarrassed that I had a pinch of skin on my back when I would have pool parties in elementary school.

As I went through puberty, I would hide my body with oversized clothing and tie shirts around my waist to cover my bum. I never wore tank tops or shorts through high school and well into my twenties. In fact, I only started wearing tank tops when I lived in Savannah, GA, and that's because it was too hot not to wear the damn tank, but it was still oversized.

This past summer I wore shorts for the first time since I was a kid, and it took me digging deep into the work I've done to feel semi-okay with showing my thighs. It was hardest in front of my family of origin – their judgment is always the deepest cut.

Apart from all of the negative messaging I received over the years, there were other, far more traumatic experiences that I believe played a big role in my discomfort with my body, the biggest being the sexual abuse that started when I was a child.

This isn't a topic that I'm going to dig deep into, as it's something that I still haven't really unpacked. The recollection of the abuse is faint, like shards of glass just beneath the skin that you can't quite get out. It was a family member, someone who was supposed to be trusted, and it carried on for years. They moved out of the city shortly after it started so geographical distance made it occur less often than I think it would have otherwise. I have occasionally shared this story with friends but I never told my own family.

Once, when I was giving an overview of my life to a fairly new therapist, she told me I was telling my story like it was someone else's – like I had no connection to it. The feelings around the trauma had been bottled up and buried so deep that I didn't have access anymore. What I do know is that it stole my sense of safety within my own body. It was once suggested that sometimes women "pad" their bodies as a way of protecting themselves. That resonated with me.

In those same early years of my childhood, my dad and his new wife moved to Boston. That abandonment left a void that I tried to fill for years through unhealthy eating behaviors, and later, through even unhealthier relationships.

My teen years were made up of a revolving door of guys. I was always looking for their approval, constantly giving away pieces of myself, thinking it was the only way I could be loved. Each destructive relationship would chip away at what little self-worth I had left. I found myself in my twenties, living independently and spiraling into some binge eating nightmares.

My first long-term adult relationship was intense. We fell in love hard and fast and I knew in my bones that it wasn't going to end well, but the passion spoke louder than the sensibility for a while. The honeymoon phase lasted six months. It was dripping with lust. It was tumultuous, but the fights would end with great sex, gifts, and promises – that I would eventually realize were very empty.

There was a lot of betrayal, abuse, and hard times, and my body image and self-worth was battered. I got a puppy as a bandaid and it was a good one for a year, then one day, I looked at her and knew that we both needed protection. I packed up my car with my dog in tow and left him while he was at work. I was broken. I couldn't eat and I started losing weight, which turned into an unhealthy obsession. I thought, *if only I was thinner, then maybe we could get back together and have a better relationship.* I also liked the attention I was getting from other men in the interim. I felt powerful and sexy.

There were only five months between the end of that relationship and meeting my husband. I met him when I was at my smallest since high school. We would go on dates and share a dessert. I feared what would happen if I gained weight again. I was nervous to let him touch my stomach and feel the stretched pouch that was tucked into my jeans. He was tender and kind. I wanted to get married. I'm not sure if it's because I knew he was a man I could love forever, because I wanted to start a family, or because I wanted him to marry me before I gained weight again... maybe all of that played a role in my sense of urgency.

We were married 13 months later with lots of leftover cupcakes. After months of wedding dress fittings, hoping that each time they would be able to take it in another inch, I wanted to eat all of the cupcakes, every last one of them. With the discovery that I was pregnant and without a need to fit into a white dress, permission to eat the cupcakes was granted. I gained 70 lbs with my first pregnancy. I remember the shame that I felt every time the OB nurse would comment on my weight gain. I felt that shame but I was able to push it aside because I felt like a goddess right up until the moment I gave birth. I wish more people had prepared me for the after-birth experience.

At a time when I didn't even recognize my body, I hated it so much and my marriage got rocky. I was completely blindsided, betrayed, and lost. But we had a baby and that baby was my whole world. I knew there was work to be done and I hoped we could do it together. Fast forward through most of my thirties, and there was a lot of the same – a lot of hurt and pain mixed with more joy and love than I ever knew existed.

It wasn't until I found myself ten years into marriage – with almost as many years of couples' therapy – realizing that I needed to put as much energy into bettering myself as I had put into bettering the marriage. And with that, I started to make changes. Not all of the changes have stuck with me, though. At first I needed to gain control over the anxiety that had taken hold of my life, and with a naturopath's guidance, I gave up refined sugar. I did it for over a year and it helped a lot. I felt good, great even. I had more energy; I was waking up early to workout; I could run a couple of blocks and fast enough that my kids were impressed; I had less brain fog, more purpose, and my anxiety was manageable.

And as much as I told myself that it wasn't about weight loss, that part was the most rewarding. I bought a whole new wardrobe and loved all the comments about how great I looked. It all fed into my early childhood messaging. I had value. I was being praised for taking care of myself, and even though I knew that people genuinely cared about that positive change, I also knew that they saw the change in my physical appearance more than they could see the change in me internally.

I couldn't stop obsessing about wanting a donut or ice cream. I would spend hours a day planning meals, baking (healthy treats) for the first time in my life, all the while wondering what I would eat on the weekend when I was allowed to "cheat." I didn't call it a cheat day because I know that language is important, but it still felt like a cheat day – and that day was all I could think about for hours and hours every week. So many wasted hours. I couldn't imagine a life where I didn't think about missing those things. When I quit smoking after 14 years, it was hard but then it was done. This was not like that; it didn't ever feel done. Our social worlds start and end with food. My husband and I identified as foodies, so how could I maintain this sugar-free life when it was everywhere and always on my mind?

Then came some pretty major stressors followed by a pandemic, and the sugar slowly crept its way back into my life, until I was out buying a whole new wardrobe again, staring at jeans that no longer fit and feeling shame when I knew that I would face people after lockdown and be judged.

So I continued the work. I worked with my therapist around body image and did some EMDR. I was reading related books, listening to podcasts, and following body positive accounts on social media. At the end of the day I often found myself conflicted with ideas and extrinsically motivated to do something. I kept seeing other women talk about accepting their fat bodies and showing off their rolls and stretch marks and in some ways that was so helpful because it allowed me to see bodies like mine – finally! In other ways, though, I had a really hard time understanding how they could just be OK with their bodies the way they were.

In one of the books I was reading, it explained how diet culture has destroyed us and if we just let ourselves eat intuitively then we wouldn't suffer from the restriction mentality. Well, let me tell you what I learned: I can eat Haagen-Dazs ice cream forever and ever in unlimited quantities and never get sick of it, ever! I'm pretty sure that's not what that book intended to teach me. So I stopped reading that book half way through.

I continued to hear women say that as soon as they accepted their bodies, they started to release weight. It sounded like a miracle – sign me up! I wanted that to happen for me. I'm still waiting…

I feel like I started conducting a science experiment, however subconsciously. I continued to let my body change. I ate the food. I binged – a lot. I started anxiety meds so that the sugar wasn't an issue for my mental health anymore. Could I sit in this place, this very hard place, without judging myself? Could I love myself even in a body I've been taught to hate? I wanted to shed the shame I felt. Maybe if I could get to a place with a little less shame, then I could release weight that wasn't tied to any exterior motivation.

Here's the thing: isn't it all about our capacity? When faced with anxiety, the rawness that comes up in a moment of true despair means getting to the next moment feeling better, whatever "better" means. For some that looks like a drink or a joint, and I've done those, too, but they don't replace my biggest addiction. They just lead me to the food, the sugar, with even less inhibitions.

My capacity for this work is a constant ebb and flow, just like my body. It is ever-changing, and that is what I am starting to understand and accept.

At this point, I can tell you two things. One – I haven't released any weight while writing this chapter, despite my hopes that writing would be a healing process moving me closer to that (misled) goal. Two – I have released some really unrealistic ideas of what beauty means. I've noticed this most in my work as a photographer. As a wedding photographer, getting a beautiful image used to always seem easier with "beautiful people." This year, I have noticed that my inspiration comes from connection – solely connection between the people I am photographing and their connection with me. Seeing two people completely in love, accepting of another person just as they are, allowing them to take up space in their heart, in their world – that is what makes a beautiful human.

As I stared at myself in a full length mirror, wearing a strappy party dress in a 2XL, I first saw a body that I wanted to pick apart. Do I look like a big Christmas tree? What about my back fat? How can I hide that? Then I started to see something different. With my hands in my pockets, I got playful and felt joy. I twirled in the dress and began to like what I saw – still with a critical eye, but I'll take the win.

There aren't many instances in my life where I look back longingly. Sure, seeing photos of my kids as babies can make my heart swell and ache all at the same time. Otherwise, I don't dwell, with one big exception: my body – and wishing I could go back to a smaller size. Wishing, like I want it to be magic, so that I can still eat the ice cream and skip the workout. Hanging onto too tight jeans, hoping I'll fit back into them one day. Then I'll have a good day or moment in a day when all the work I've done – all of the growth to change my thought patterns – pays off, and I know that I am not defined by my body.

Part of my healing has been actively pushing myself outside of my comfort zone by doing things that I would have shied away from in the past, like wearing a bikini in front of friends, putting myself out there on social media as a plus-sized woman who still loves fashion despite the fact that fashion doesn't always love us, and a big one was doing a boudoir shoot with my husband. I booked a boudoir shoot as a way of pushing myself deeper into the journey while writing this chapter. The first thought that crossed my mind the minute after I confirmed was *what can I do to be thinner by then?* The shoot was only two weeks away, so there was absolutely nothing I could do but force myself to stay with those hard feelings, and accept my body for what it was in that moment; that was the whole point. I knew that I wasn't going to love every image, but I needed to see myself in that light. A woman who is desired by her husband. A woman who can feel sexy in lace. A woman who doesn't need anyone's approval to exist in her own body. So I wrote out some notes to myself about what I know makes me feel good AND I also binged on ice cream as I fell back into disordered eating habits. These things are hard-wired, and as I am working to untwist those tangled wires, there's always another knot to get through.

The day came to do the boudoir shoot, and my body almost rejected the whole thing. I was exhausted; so tired that I took a nap, which was completely out of the ordinary for me. I slept until the last possible minute and was grateful that I had booked hair and makeup because I showed up a hot mess. She did her magic and I left feeling a little more able to take on what was ahead. The shoot was amazing and I felt empowered. My husband and I took away an incredible experience. I actually felt like I didn't want to see the photos; the fact that I did it was all I needed, and in my mind I was worried that the photos would ruin it for me. They didn't! Out of the 100 images, I absolutely loved at least 7, and cringed at many others, but holy shit, I LOVED some. That's life! Some moments you will feel sexy and empowered and others will be less than desired. Learning that I don't have to love all of the individual parts of my body to accept it as a whole – has been the biggest turning point for me.

I caught a glimpse of myself in a window today as I was walking to get coffee. I wondered if my outfit made me look huge. It's for this reason that I don't have any full length mirrors in my bedroom. I can't trust myself yet. I focus on how I feel in my clothes - I want to feel fashionable, comfortable,

IT FELT GOOD TO FINALLY, TRULY, SEE MYSELF FOR WHO I AM AND NOT WHAT I *weigh.*

and confident. I rely on my internal feelings and not the lies that the mirror tells me. Shopping is hard. Often I will skip the changing room altogether. I am the queen of returns, after all. I bring it home and see how it feels without the harsh judgment of a changing room mirror.

Yes, you are right; this all sounds a lot like I am still on this roller coaster ride of body acceptance. I am 100% sure that I always will be, but I also see how far I've come. I'm writing this chapter right now, showing up, being vulnerable, and facing the fuckery of it all. That's a lot further than previous generations have come, which also means there is hope for my daughter and hypothetical grandkids. Perhaps all of our unlearning means that they will have a little less struggle and more love for themselves, just as they are.

I've talked to my daughter about body image, and she thinks that I am comfortable as I am. As she gets older, I will let her see more of the complexity behind my body acceptance, but in her formative years, I wanted her to see confidence. I wanted her to have positive messaging even if that wasn't always what was going on inside my head. I never wanted her to hear how hateful I could be towards myself, because that was a broken part of me that needed (and still needs) healing. It's a part of her that I hope never breaks. A girl's confidence can start to plummet around age 10. She is now 12, and still confident AF. That tells me that I've done something right.

# Chapter 2

## AMANDA CASE

Author Photo: Alicia Thurston
www.mvpmeals.com | IG:@amandacatherinec

### EARLY DAYS

I grew up in one of the most beautiful places I've ever been to: a tiny town called Jeffreys on the east coast of Canada, in the province of Newfoundland, close to the ocean with beautiful scenic mountains that I didn't appreciate until I grew up and went back to visit. It was a town so quiet and rural that the nearest hospital was an hour drive and all students from kindergarten to grade 12 went to the same school. I was a super shy, awkward, and chubby kid. My mom dressed me from the very high end place known as Salvation Army. No outfit was complete without my oversized dorky, coke bottle glasses. We struggled financially, and as a result, we ate a lot of processed, unhealthy food. We were blessed, however, with parents who were kind and full of love and valued a daily, home cooked, family sit-down dinner; it's a tradition that I still keep. My parents were great cooks. I became a foodie at a young age.

The first time I ever thought about my body and what other people think of it was when a boy at school poked my belly and said "just like the Pillsbury dough boy!"

I was mortified by all the kids laughing at me and I felt so ashamed. At this point, I started getting teased and body comments from kids and also family. Even the seemingly harmless comments such as, "She must love food!" "Look at all that baby weight. Don't worry, you will drop that one day," stung deep and made me start thinking that something was wrong or bad about my body.

As a pre-teen, I became self-conscious and focused on body image. All I saw was a fat, ugly person in the mirror. I was sick of being an ugly duckling, and I wanted to become one of the "hot" girls. I started working out every day. There were no gyms where I lived, so I jogged daily and followed along to Richard Simmons' or Denise Richards' aerobic tape that my Aunt was so kind to lend me. To this day, I still think of the impact and how pivotal those fitness tapes became in my life. Not only were they one of the few resources that I had available to me to become healthier and hotter, but they were one of the few resources that I had for an outlet to deal with difficult family dynamics that were stressful. I buried myself in school work and working out. Seeing the change in my body and the great comments from people reinforced the messaging of how much more liked and desirable I was, only when my body was smaller.

As another way to control my body and stay skinny, I obsessively started counting calories. I ate as little as possible and remembered asking the nutrition teacher if "bodies can survive if we just take vitamins instead of eating real food." *Insert facepalm emoji*. With such a strict diet and workout regimen, control was important. I started forming a pattern where I would crave certain "bad" foods and binge on occasion. This started seeming like the perfect solution to stay skinny. I thought to myself that I would eat healthy foods as much as possible, but when I couldn't resist bad food, I would purge it out of my body and I wouldn't get fat. I was so terrified of being fat again that I said to myself as a teenage girl that I would rather die than be fat EVER again.

I started realizing that maybe I was not in a healthy place when I was borderline anorexic and I still saw a huge chubby kid in the mirror. Hello, body dysmorphia.

Once I finished high school, I left Newfoundland and moved to Ontario. I got my first job at a Wendy's restaurant in Stratford, Ontario. At this age, being hot and skinny was everything. My obsession with exercising and eating a certain way was still mainly motivated by being "hot and skinny," but it also started becoming about health and wellness. I lost my Dad and Grandmother to heart attacks and alcoholism. His mother, my other grandma, was diagnosed with breast cancer. These tragedies made me realize how important our health is. I became more into health and fitness – not only for myself now, but I started wanting to teach other people what I learned and loved.

I wanted to find a way to work for this calling. I got a job at an exclusively women's gym. That's when I realized that I could make a career out of exercising, eating healthily, and helping other people. The owners of the gym made it very clear that in order to work there you had to look a certain way and maintain a certain body image. I studied kinesiology and physical education. While I went to school, I worked in a gym as a personal trainer and taught fitness classes at a different, more inclusive women's gym. I absolutely loved this gym. I continued to restrict food items, count calories, and teach fitness classes. Back then I thought I was working in this field because it was my passion, but looking back I realize that it was also part of a way to control my body. If I worked in the industry, I got paid to workout and I could stay skinny and obsessed with controlling how I looked. With so much pressure to be fit as a personal trainer and fitness instructor, surely I would stay skinny and healthy and not "let myself go." As long as I stayed small (which I did), I was happy. I based my happiness and self-worth on the size of my body and how FIT I looked. I convinced myself that nobody wanted to take a fitness class, personal training session, or nutrition consult from someone who did not appear as though they walked the talk.

## MOTHERHOOD

Stepping into motherhood was such an exciting time and so full of happiness since I always knew that I wanted to be a mother. In the back of my mind, my inner critic, hater voice was still there, reminding me that pregnancy means a bigger body, which is less desirable. I had anxiety about gaining all that weight, having my body out of control, and what other people would say if I didn't immediately snap back to a fit, slim body. I ate healthily, worked out, was concerned about gaining weight and controlling to a point – but I wanted a healthy pregnancy so I made sure that I ate more of a well-balanced diet. It was very difficult at times, but amazing at other times just to feel your body doing all of these magical things to bring another life into this world. Yet, I still focused on avoiding unnecessary weight gain. It's so sad to remember how much energy I wasted worrying about the size of my body instead of being in body bliss bringing my beautiful daughters into this world. I wish I would have been kinder to myself during this major transition.

I wanted to breastfeed for my daughters' health but I have to admit that I also wanted to do this because it would help me drop the baby weight, or at least that's what everyone said. I was eager to get back to working out as well. With a baby who was colicky and never slept, I remember feeling shitty for all the times I said to personal training clients who were moms, that those who claim it's so hard after kids were just using this as an excuse. **Another major facepalm emoji**. I can't believe that I used to believe that. Here I was with a loving, supportive husband, able to take maternity leave, and I was struggling to get a shower in daily, let alone eat perfectly within my macros and fit in consistent workouts. When I did work out, I barely made it through. I wish I had given myself more compassion back then. I wish I would have told myself that it was okay to skip the gym this week, or go ahead and eat that donut. I wish I had told myself that it was okay to not be perfect and it was okay to gain weight and not "snap back." I really wanted to prove to myself that I could be a mom that did not let herself go and stayed skinny and pretty.

## PCOS DIAGNOSIS

With two daughters, a husband, a full time career, and a thriving business, I was go go go! I still kept my health a top priority – after all, I was a Wellness Consultant, and I have to practise what I preach. I was working out 3-5 days a week, eating a restricted diet, taking my supplements, drinking the water, and *doing* the damn thang! I had a more balanced approach to eating but still restricted, yet I was gaining weight… and at the time, this was horrific to me!

I realized that the only way I could stay slim was by following a severely restricted diet and exercising regularly. Otherwise, I gained weight even if what I ate was healthy. From my health background, I knew that wasn't 'normal' and that there was definitely a deeper issue that was hormone-related. I went to my doctor and my naturopath, because clearly if I was gaining weight and doing all the things, something was wrong with me. My doctor diagnosed me with PCOS and put me on metformin and birth control. I didn't have any results with those except a more regular period. I went to see a naturopath who put me on the natural route with lifestyle changes and supplements. MORE WORK on the full plate of an exhausted person. The naturopath and my doctor also confirmed I had a genetic gluten allergy from a celiac family. The plot thickens.

Okay, I had tried the medicine, tried the natural lifestyle changes, and I was still up and down in my body. I went on living frustrated daily, with facial hair, blood sugar fluctuations, weight gain up and down, irregular periods, and living with body image issues related to all of those things. I had to do the work daily. I was feeling exhausted and so frustrated that I could eat and workout perfectly all week, then eat ONE carb-heavy meal on a weekend and I would be up 10 pounds on the scale on Monday. Then I would spend the week undoing that damage. It was exhausting. I've never been a jealous person, but I got so frustrated with my body that I would be so irritated and jealous of my friends who could eat normally and not be overweight and the ones who ate whatever they wanted, when they wanted, and stayed skinny.

## THE PRESSURE OF THE FITNESS INDUSTRY

Working in the fitness industry, I was very eager to drop that baby weight due to the high pressure in this industry to "snap back," or I was not healthy, and therefore not worthy of being a Personal Trainer or Fitness Instructor. I dropped some of that weight, yet I was down on myself for not losing the 50+ pounds that I had gained. Exhausted with working, mom life and starting my business, MVP Meals, I was less strict with my "plan," so I gained more weight and the scale went over 200 pounds again. I was not happy with the number on the scale, but this was the beginning of me feeling like I just wanted to be free. I was sooooo sick and exhausted from dieting, sick of the pressure, sick of never feeling slim enough or happy with my body, sick of avoiding social gatherings out of fear of falling off track and gaining weight. I was sick of it all. I wanted to feel free and no longer be a prisoner in my own body!

Around this time, the beginning of the body positivity movement started. I started reading and digging deep as to WHY having a body that's as small as possible was so important to me. Where did I learn this? What if I freed myself? What if I allowed myself to enjoy food and miss leg day? What if I gained 100 lbs and still felt like the same person? What would happen if I gained 100 lbs? How would I feel? How would life be different?

I started realizing when I looked in my daughters' eyes that I didn't want that for them. I didn't want their self-worth to be determined by how they look. Knowing that I was their biggest role model, I had to change. I had to change what I believed about beauty. I had to change what I believed about myself. I had to change what I believed about my self-worth. I had to change what I said out loud. I had to change what I said to my daughters about self-love, self-worth, and body acceptance. I have two little girls growing up in this world. I want them to have a solid foundation of their self-worth, confidence, and healthy body image. So how do I do that when my own body image is struggling?

First of all, where did I even learn this nonsense that became so real that as a young woman I told myself I'd rather die than get *fat*. WHAAAAT?! Where did I learn that bigger bodies are unworthy? Where did I learn that if I don't look a certain way, I am not worthy of working in the fitness industry? Where did I learn that a woman has to have the same body that she had before giving birth? I had to dig deep as to where these beliefs came from, and I had to challenge them. I started opening my eyes, reading, unlearning, and listening to other women and leaders of the body positivity movement. I felt a shift. I started learning about self-growth, personal development, mindest, affirmations, meditations, cord cutting, etc. I practised all of it and started to shift my own beliefs. I challenged other people on these beliefs as well. I realized how much those beliefs, as real and prevalent as they are, are FULL OF SHIT! I started shifting not only my thoughts, but the conversations that I had with other people. I shut down comments about mine and my daughters' bodies and set boundaries, advising people to focus on non-appearance-based compliments.

## LEARNING TO LOVE MYSELF

In learning to love myself in my late twenties by working on my triggers and mindset, I got to a place where I never stepped on a scale. I stopped bingeing when I ate bad food after my first daughter. I stopped counting calories. I approached health more holistically and focused on healing all of the damage I've done from extreme dieting and exercising. I made eating well, exercising regularly, hydration, stress reduction, and sleep priorities. I felt great and more confident than ever. I took care of myself well and felt more connected to myself and more in love with my body than ever. I was in a really good place. I had days where I felt fat. Then I talked myself out of that. I used positive affirmations, journaling, and meditation to retrain my brain. I read books. At this point, I had really embraced my curves and no longer wanted to lose weight. I was enjoying life and being in the present moment. I was surrounding myself with like minded women who were truly confident in their skin.

My self-love game was on fleek. I looked in the mirror and didn't see an overweight, unworthy woman. I looked in the mirror and saw a *Bad Bitch*! I saw a devoted mother and wife, a woman who went for her dreams and runs a successful business that makes others' lives easier. I saw a kind person who would do anything for the ones she loves. I saw a bubbly, outgoing, positive people-person. I saw a growth-focused person who prioritizes learning and pours into those around me to lift them up. I saw a great cook, a pretty face, a pretty soul. I saw someone who was bold and brave. Someone who loves nature and playing guitar. **It felt good to finally, truly, SEE myself for who I am and not what I weigh.** My plan was to move as much as possible, eat to nourish and enjoy food, and wherever my body sits, well, that's where it's meant to be. No more stressing about weight or food or exercise.

## HANDLING TRIGGERS

Just when I thought that my days of body esteem issues were over, I started struggling with acne and rashes from the extreme stress of business and separating with my husband. My face was so full of cystic acne that not even makeup would cover it up, and some days it was so bad that I couldn't even wear makeup. I started to feel so ugly. It was a huge trigger for me. At least at this point in my life I had gained so much confidence that it had less of an impact, but it still had an impact on my happiness and desire to put myself out there. I went back to doing the work and got control of the acne.

Next up to test how far I had come with my body bliss, was...drumroll, pleaseeee...the Covid-19 pandemic hit and the world was shaken upside down. My life was also shaken upside down. My business scaled way back, I was homeschooling our children, there was less movement, more stress, more indulging in alcohol, and more indulging in snacks and sweets. When the gyms opened back up and I decided to weigh myself, I had gained 45 or more pounds since I had last weighed myself two years prior. I was SHOCKED, angry, and bitter. I was so disappointed in myself for allowing myself to not only gain that much weight, but for also being heavier than my heaviest pregnancy weight. I had officially gained over 100 pounds since my husband and I had met 15 years ago. Then my inner hater came back stronger than ever. Was he still attracted to me? Do I still even look healthy? What do people think when they look at me now? Would they think that I had "let myself go"? I started hating my chubby face. I felt depressed and unmotivated for the first time ever. I had no energy for my kids or business. I didn't recognize myself. I looked into plastic surgery but was too overweight even for that. I took a trip and could barely fit in the seatbelt.

My worst nightmare had come true. I was FAT. I looked in the mirror and no longer saw the bad bitch. I saw the chubby, unpopular, nerdy, shy kid staring back at me. Some days I could barely get out of bed with the combination of the pandemic stress and my weight gain stress. For the first time in my life of 35 years, I was battling depression. I was struggling to stay afloat and not drown. My mental health was the worst it had ever been. Determined to not stay in this awful space, I had to push through and deal with it. I had to go back and do all the work again. This time it was easier since I had a good foundation from past inner work, and I had a mindset shift again.

I thought long and hard about body image, confidence, self-esteem, inner work, and self-acceptance. I realized that it's a myth that we cannot simultaneously love ourselves and want to improve ourselves. I had grown to love myself as a person. I had a temporary relapse, but I got back on track. I wrote down my goals along with the "why" and "how" behind them. I realized that I could love myself the same despite how skinny, fat, motivated, or depressed I was. I can learn to love myself through whatever I am going through because I've given myself one of the most important life changing gifts: the tools for self-love and body acceptance.

Anybody who says that weight doesn't impact health is dead wrong. Although I promote loving yourself no matter where your body is at, I also promote health. From someone who was very slim and active to someone who was less active and overweight, the weight affected my health, energy, fashion, my business, marriage, and relationship with my kids. It's not to say that you can't be overweight and still be healthy, because I have worked with a lot of overweight fit people who are killing it, yet by the outdated BMI scale, a doctor would say they are morbidly obese. (That's a topic that I have a lot to say about, but will save that for another day.)

At least now I realize the importance of a balanced approach to sustainable weight maintenance for healthy living. Obsessively controlling our bodies to a point of negative impact on our lives is not healthier or better than neglecting our self-care because society says being skinny is always better and healthier. I can tell you firsthand from being on both extremes that they both suck. Finding equilibrium somewhere in the middle is important AF.

## LESSONS LEARNED

Here is what I've learned and what I would like to pass on to my daughters and every woman who struggles with body image. Having a good body image starts with accepting and liking your body exactly as it is, even if you want to improve certain areas. We can't wait until a body part is perfect for us to like it and accept ourselves. That's when our body image and self-esteem gets damaged and that affects relationships, opportunities, and health. I believe we should look into the character of a person and ourselves, rather than the size and shape of something so ever-changing as the weight and size of a body. Oftentimes these things are out of our control and are not even meant to be highly controlled.

Start the journey by digging deep to understand why you have body image issues and what is true vs. what is a story in your head that either you or someone else put there. Have a list of things that you love about your body and yourself to look at often. Have a game plan for handing that inner hater and inner mean girl by redirecting negative thoughts and energy that creep in about yourself. They are stories that are not even true. We create stories about ourselves and have to retrain our brains and work on that daily.

Pour on the self-love in your love language often: words of affirmation, acts of service, physical touch, gifts, quality time. Weight will never equal or define our worth or our health. Every time you catch yourself thinking or saying something negative about yourself, immediately stop and replace it with something positive. Nobody has to or can live up to the beauty standards of fake, highly edited people, so completely shut down the comparison game altogether. We are all different with different genetics, so it is impossible for us all to look the same way to fit in. Our children are observing and absorbing how we look at and talk about ourselves as well as others. Don't say anything about yourself or your kids that you wouldn't want them to say back.

Finally, always remember that recovery from eating disorders, body dysmorphia, poor body image, etc. is ongoing hard work and ever-evolving.

It's not a one-and-done type of deal. There will be great days, bad days, and there are definitely going to be mega triggers in your life right when you think your self-love is like Fort Knox. When the inner hater comes back, go back to the tools and do the work. Love yourself more than anybody else could ever love you. In a society that profits off of and wants you in a state of self-loathing, unconditional self-love is how you conquer and win body bliss.

# *Chapter 3*

## AMIE MARIANA SIDER

AUTHOR PHOTO:MARIANGELICA FORERO
amiemariana.com | IG: @practicalpcos

One of the best things to come out of the pandemic was my husband's and my discovery of the television show, "Alone." In case you're not familiar with this reality series, please allow me to enlighten you. The show brilliantly combines outdoor survivalism with the reality of social isolation (probably why we resonated with it so much during not one but two provincial quarantines). The ten survivalists selected are plopped into northern and remote locations with no camera crew, no team, and no producers, just their own Go-Pro type cameras and a mission to simply stay alive. $500,000 is awarded to the person who can last the longest and conquer not only the elements, but also their own personal demons.

Season eight took place in what was said to be the most dangerous location yet, the Canadian wilderness on the shores of Chilko Lake, British Columbia. Instead of enduring the usual pains like hunger, loneliness, and the elements, they also faced the deadliest predator known to North America: the grizzly bear. At the beginning of the season, we were on the edge of our comfy couch every single episode. If I had nail polish on, I had most certainly picked it off by the end of those 60 minutes.

As time went on, Matt and I actually ended up a little disappointed with the season. In no way am I trying to throw any shade at these brave participants, but we sat and observed the season almost come to a halt, simply because many of them were unable to hunt and gather or perform any other type of survivalist missions due to the impending danger. Everyone was so scared of the presence of the bears that it almost paralyzed them into a state of inaction, and the audience essentially watched them starve their way to the finish line.

How well do you know your "bears"?

Do you know them at all?

I like to think that I've always known my big grizzly because it's followed me my entire life and I have slowly but surely been working my way into coexistence with it since I was a young girl. I had no idea just how many bears I would encounter along life's path. Some of them would just glance at me briefly, leaving me only slightly stunned and thankful that they decided to move along. Some would force me to play dead, and others charged at me directly, leaving me in physical and emotional turmoil for days and years to come.

Are these bears a looming threat? Or are they simply just a part of our natural world, and we're bound to encounter them at one point or another? I'm here to tell you that you don't have to be preyed upon, and you don't have to live in crippling fear, because guess what? We can overcome or coexist with the hurts and fears of our past (our bears). I'm here to serve as a living reminder that growth is possible in the wake of trauma.

Yes, this book is about bodies, but I can't write a chapter about my body without bringing up the bears. The "bears" are simply my metaphor for my own inner demons and negative dialogue; they are also my trauma points, pain points, and my triggers. Without them, I wouldn't be able to understand my body and mind on a higher level or recognize its connectivity and how it came into its current existence. I also want to leave a content warning that this chapter discusses complex themes surrounding adoption, racism, sexual assault, and traumatic birth. Please feel free to engage or disengage as needed. With that said, let's dive in. I'm ready for you to meet my bears.

I was born in Amatitlán, Guatemala, a beautiful remote fishing village that has, unfortunately, experienced a great deal of environmental and social degradation since I was born back in 1987. I come from a strong Mayan bloodline also making me part of Guatemala's Indigenous population. I also happen to be the 13th of 18 children born to my birth mother, and the only one that she parted ways with by placing me in the care of a Canadian family via international adoption. Even though I'm currently a mother in my 30s while I write this, I still can't even begin to imagine the true weight of this life-altering decision for her. She battled abject poverty and turned to a life of drugs, crime, and prostitution just to survive.

What I'm about to write, I've never even said out loud before, so in the name of authenticity, let's continue on with this cathartic release. I have always been ashamed of my birth mother. Not because of what she did, but because of how she looked. Again, not because of her lifestyle or choices, but because of her body, her bone structure, and how looking at her somehow made me feel shame. If I dig way back into my earliest memories, I can still remember my parents sitting me on my bed in my pretty pink room as they handed me a small framed photo of her for the very first time. She was likely in her late twenties or early thirties when the photo was taken. I was about four years old when my parents gave it to me. We all thought I was ready for this special moment because from a very young age I was mature, inquisitive, and insightful with a fundamental strength beyond my years.

As an adult observer of this memory, I am heartbroken by the stark reality that my four-year-old self already possessed such a strong Western construct of beauty. It was a construct so strong that I would continually compare and contrast myself to it for the rest of my life. Seeing my birth mother's photo instantly made me feel embarrassed and ashamed that I had come from her. She was probably just shy of 5 feet tall with dark brown skin, distinct Mayan features, long black hair tied away from her face, and a very pronounced midsection. Her body looked like it was blanketed with an indescribable heaviness and sadness. My parents told me that I could put the photo wherever I wanted to. For the longest time, I simply hid it in a drawer, buried underneath my other possessions.

I would continue to bury the shame and guilt from that day for the rest of my life. I buried it with an incredibly complex relationship with food and with my body. I also took every opportunity to bury myself with whatever I could to not be fully seen. No matter what, I just didn't want the world to see me the way I saw her. Looking back, I'm not sure whether it was because I didn't feel a connection to her or if I just knew that if this photo was a crystal ball in any sort of way, I didn't want to live with the fear that her haunting look may one day become my own.

None of this made sense to me until my maternity leave with my first and only son. I needed to find a show to help pass those late nights and seemingly all-night feeding sessions. For some reason I stumbled upon *This Is Us*. Let this be a friendly disclaimer to anyone reading and thinking about starting this show. Do not watch *This Is Us* if you are pregnant, postpartum, pms-ing, or basically anything else to do with hormones and the letter P. I would sit and cry a steady stream of tears all over my sweet little newborn's chubby round face every single episode.

That show shook me to my core not just because of the ongoing evolution surrounding its origin story of adoption, but also because of how Randall Pearson's character develops at every physical and emotional age and stage, as he grows up as the only black and adopted child in an all-white family. One of Randall's lines from Season 3 served as the biggest "a-ha" moment for me when he said, "It has defined my life, being adopted. It has defined my life, even when I didn't realize it was defining it. And I think a part of that, at least for me, is that this big giant thing happened to me, and I didn't have any say in it." That's exactly it; this huge, life-altering event happened to us and we had zero say in it. This is also known as trauma. Trauma takes away your choice and no matter when trauma happens to you (and trust me, it will), it's usually out of your control. No matter how successful or amazing my life turned out to be, it still started with what felt like rejection and resulted in a baby girl coming to Canada under refugee status about to have her world rocked by Western society at large. This will always be my greatest blessing and biggest bear.

Let's rewind back to my puberty days. Puberty sucks for everyone, and I mean EVERYONE. It doesn't matter who you are or where you came from. You simply can't escape the extreme awkwardness, pain, angst, and all of the ungodly sights, smells, and emotions during those pre-teen and teen years. Navigating this delicate time was extra difficult as I began to grow in my own awareness of what it actually means to be a woman within the BIPOC (Black, Indigenous, and other People of Colour) community. People often project the arrival of womanhood onto girls experiencing their first menstrual bleed. Mine happened to come at the ripe age of ten years old. Even though my body met all of the physical requirements, I was far from a woman. I was still a child just going about my existence in a small, conservative (and predominantly Caucasian) town. For the sake of time, let's skip all of the intentional and unintentional acts of racism that I experienced in that town from kindergarten, onward. I'll save those bears for my future autobiography (insert wink face here).

It was the day of our winter assembly and every class had to prepare a song and skit. That day also happened to fall on our school's monthly McDonald's lunch day. I got my usual order of chicken McNuggets and enjoyed my fried food bliss before the assembly started. A few acts before our turn, I started getting strange pains. I awkwardly made my way to the back of the gym to find my teacher and asked to use the washroom. I assumed my discomfort was due to a "bad" chicken nugget. I was shocked to see my trendy white cargo pants full of blood. Yes...white cargo pants on school assembly day that were stained with my bright red blood from that damn chicken nugget! Don't worry, after a few moments of panic and silence, I was able to determine that this was the poorly timed work of Mother Nature instead of McDonald's.

The presence of my period brought new and surprising challenges like boobs, body hair, hips, and hormones. Seriously, no one should be forced to go to school during puberty. Since I developed a little earlier than some of my peers, I began to attract what is known in feminist theory as the male gaze. If you need a quick crash course, the male gaze is simply a perversion of our biological drive to find a potential mate. It twists that natural process and instead turns women into passive items to possess and use, creating an overtly sexualized object for male desire. After everything I've experienced in my lifetime, let me assure you that the male gaze is just as terrifying and unwanted as the gaze of a 600-pound grizzly.

I don't think I can confidently say that I ever understood my body or made decisions about it under my own terms until recently. It always felt like some external source was telling me how to feel, what to wear, what to emphasize, and what to hide. This was consistent for me through every life stage from puberty to adolescence, and adulthood all the way to motherhood. I became a passive observer instead of an active participant in the narrative surrounding my body. As a direct result, I put my body under all kinds of scrutiny just to keep myself from standing out, drawing uninvited attention, and being referred to as "exotic." Although many people innocently thought that it was a genuine compliment, being referred to as exotic is actually more of a backhanded compliment. It's one that serves as a harsh reminder that BIPOC women are not the standard, because how we look is somehow less real and less respectable than White folks. Exotic makes me a little less human, a little more primitive, and even animalistic. Exotic makes me easier to be preyed upon, traded, collected, and showcased. I am none of these things but I am everything to me and to those who will come after me, and my sacred beauty will always be defined on my own terms.

My university years held three deliberate occurrences of sexual assault. I've decided that no one needs the full details and backdrop except for my therapist and me. I'm simply not ready to share all of the specifics surrounding my sexual pain and trauma. We certainly need to believe women, but I also think that it's just as important that we not dismiss women if they are not ready to unearth or relive that trauma. These events changed who I am completely and have left me with compounding physical and emotional destruction that I'm still working hard to rebuild every single day. Combatting the deep shame around each incident of trauma feels like a full-time job.

You see, there's a huge difference between guilt and shame. Guilt says, "I made a mistake," where shame says, "I am the mistake." When the brain is faced with shame, it responds the same way it would to a physical threat because it's telling us that something is wrong; there's a total lack of safety, and therefore I need to fight or flee. Trust me, I've done my fair share of both. If you're reading this, you probably have too.

I see you.

These assaults left me feeling empty and alone. Both of my best friends at the time had moved out west, so I didn't have my usual support system in place. Even though my parents were always some of my best and most trusted friends, I didn't want to bring them into the equation – not out of fear of judgment, but I just didn't want them to hurt like I was hurting. I didn't want them to feel bad for me or to take it upon themselves to seek some kind of justice. That's the funny thing about shame. It likes to keep you in the darkness and easily convinces you not to give it light. As Brene Brown says, "If you put shame in a Petri dish, it needs three things to grow exponentially: secrecy, silence, and judgment. If you put the same amount of shame in a Petri dish and douse it with empathy, it can't survive."

Since I didn't seek professional help until many years later, I acquired my own coping mechanisms. Food quickly became my biggest comfort and escape. Not only did I put on 30 pounds in about three months, but I also became addicted to the act of filling myself with food to avoid feeling empty.

These disordered relationships stemmed from my desire to physically protect myself and avoid feelings of emptiness and loneliness. The drastic weight gain became my shield of choice and I hid behind it constantly. Someone once made a comment in my presence stating that rape was the ultimate compliment because it boils down to someone wanting you so badly that they had to go to extreme and illegal lengths just to have you. If you are a sexual assault survivor or know one, you'll understand how shame-enforcing and downright disgusting that comment was to me. At the same time, I think I also took it as advice. If my body was getting me into all this trouble for looking a certain way, then maybe my body could help me do the opposite. I proceeded to eat whatever I was craving in extreme quantities in order to wear my excess weight as a shield.

I used to binge my way to extreme physical discomfort and even pain. I never purged because that little voice inside of me told me that I deserved to sit in the excruciating pain that came with the fullness. Holding onto food or weight definitely fills a void. Whenever I felt empty or lonely, food was always there to keep me company and fill me right to the brim. In case you're wondering, you can still feel lonely even if you live in a house full of people. You can still feel unworthy and undeserving of health and happiness regardless of the company you keep when you live with unresolved trauma.

Given my birth mother's remarkable number of children, pregnancy was always my number one fear. As a teenager, I had myself convinced that I was so naturally fertile that I would likely get pregnant just by looking at someone the wrong way.

I finally met a man who saw me the way I needed to be seen and was my match in so many ways. Once we had been married for a few years we were ready to "start trying" for a baby. I was shocked to find out that it wouldn't be that simple for me. I was officially diagnosed with PCOS (Polycystic Ovarian Syndrome) in 2014 and I was devastated. PCOS is a hormone and metabolic disorder. The symptoms widely differ between women and people with PCOS, but the three main areas affected are fertility and reproductive health, metabolic health, and psychological health. There is no known cure for PCOS but with a lot of hard work and dedication, symptoms can be managed over time.

I probably should've known it was coming. I had the hallmark symptoms like irregular periods, missing periods, and I once had a period that I couldn't get stopped for over three weeks. My cycles were always irregular, ovulation was always painful (almost more so than my actual period), and

I battled cystic acne, excess body hair, weight gain, and uncontrollable appetite. If that wasn't enough, severe depression and anxiety surfaced a few months prior to my diagnosis as well. It's probably one of the most unsexy and embarrassing disorders to talk about, and now it's all I do.

Matt and I had given up all hope of becoming pregnant on our own. We weren't ready to pursue IVF, adoption, or any other alternatives. We didn't want to make a big deal about it; we just quietly kept it between us while also trying to convince ourselves that we didn't actually need children.

One beautiful fall day, I was on a walk with one of my best friends and she shared that she was pregnant with her second child. She was listing off some of her body's physical pains and discomforts and I was empathizing a little too enthusiastically. She chuckled at my responses and asked if I thought I might be pregnant too. I assured her that pregnancy wasn't possible for me right now so there was no way. It was likely just work stress or fatigue. After our walk, I jokingly said that I needed to go home and take a nap and then I'll do a pregnancy test. To my shock, the test came back positive so I immediately sent her the photo of my completed test just to make sure I wasn't seeing things.

My pregnancy was hard. I was an anxious mess the entire time, so much so that it was almost impossible for me to enjoy any of it. I felt like my physical and emotional body was at capacity at all times. During my sixth week of pregnancy, I had some spotting and intense cramping. I thought I was losing the baby. We went to the ER where they spoke to me in such a cold, matter- of-fact way and told me that my yoke sack was empty and that it was within my best interest to proceed with a D & C procedure to clear everything out and start again. We went home feeling defeated. We did what we always do in a crisis and turned to family, our support network of friends, and did a lot of praying and discussing.

We came to the conclusion that we wanted to ask for more blood work instead of booking the D & C. We wanted to see if my HCG levels would go up on their own first. As I went into the blood lab at the hospital, one of the nurses there just so happened to be my friend's mom. She comforted me, said a quick prayer, and I sat and waited to get my blood drawn. While I was waiting, another one of my best friend's daughters sent me the most beautiful little voice note singing the "yeah yeah" song – one that Matt and I had made up while playing with her. As soon as I heard it, I knew everything was going to be okay. The tests confirmed that my levels were up and that there was a sweet little someone growing inside of me fighting for their chance to be known.

My son's entire birth story is one that I'm still not ready to share in full, due to the layered complexity of both medical and racial trauma. At the end of my pregnancy we knew that something wasn't right. My body had begun to swell at alarming rates. My son was due on the 26th of May (a Thursday), but by the Sunday of the long weekend, I experienced rapid weight gain, my hands were so swollen that I was unable to make a fist, and I had headaches so bad that I could barely muster the strength to move. We tried calling the midwife and the on-call system, but they said they were already too busy with other births and I would have to wait until Tuesday to be seen by someone. We were assured that swelling was normal and we could go to the ER if we felt otherwise, but were also reminded that we would be discharged from their care if we did so.

I guess we just tried to be compliant as best we could. After all, this was our first time experiencing all this. On Tuesday, we went in and they told us they were too busy once again. This time all the midwives could physically see my swollen face and limbs and I was still denied care. Matt was visibly frustrated and scared, and I began to sob. Matt was advocating for me hardcore as they tried to assure him we just needed to wait a little longer. I remember him telling them that I didn't have a little longer and that he was going to take me straight to the hospital if they tried to refuse to support me one more time. I guess we were both loud enough that the only Latina midwife on staff heard us. She came out and took one quick look at my hands and feet and yelled, "This woman needs help immediately!" She was actually off the clock that day and still brought us into her office, took my vitals, and sent us on our way to the nearest hospital.

Once there, I was diagnosed with preeclampsia and they started to induce labor by inserting a hormone strip up into my vagina. The on-call doctor was a large man who probably stood at about 6'4, and for some reason his physical size and especially his hand size was a trigger for me while he attempted to insert this hormone strip up into my vaginal canal. I had a panic attack and was terrified and mortified all at once. I remember begging for a woman to please switch with him to do this job but my request was denied, so I did the best I could to endure the process while crying in pain the entire time.

There were multiple other racial microaggressions taken toward me that day from both the midwives and hospital staff. I even had a visit from family and children's services because of my breakdown and they wanted to ensure that I was going to be a safe parent to my newborn. I was made to feel like this birth was somehow a burden on the system and that no one really wanted me there or thought that I was competent enough to do this. I had no makeup on and I was so swollen that I barely had any remnants of a face. I am convinced that the only reason I was able to receive even a mediocre standard of care was due to the presence of my white husband and white parents. Thankfully, they all advocated for me hardcore the entire time. They were afraid for my safety too. I ended up needing an emergency C-section to help deliver my son. There was a shift change just before my delivery and my final nurse was a beautiful and kind Black woman who treated me with respect, dignity, and care. She stood around the bed with Matt and my parents and said a prayer over me before heading to the operating room. I'm still not entirely sure if she was real or an angel.

It was time to flip the script. I've been seeing bears my entire life, but with the birth of my son, Orson Wilder, I went from seeing bears to seeing my baby bear. Trauma transforms us. My big scary bears evolved into something different when I held my own sweet little bear in my arms for the first time. He was living and breathing proof that I had overcome my darkest demons and that I was worthy of his love and his presence. Orson's birth story showed my inner strength like I had never seen it before. I was strong, I was beautiful, and I was resilient.

The name Orson means bear. In the kingdom of spirit animals, the bear is emblematic of grounding forces and strength. The bear is revered as a powerful totem to those who need the courage to stand up against adversity. The bear exists as a powerful guide to support physical and emotional healing and encourages those who have experienced its healing abilities to go and help others. That's my boy; that's my bear.

Transformation is possible. Transformation comes with resilience and a lifetime of work. Your transformation probably won't look like mine, and that's okay. Becoming a parent helped me understand the true necessity of seeking healing and therapy for all my trauma bears. I continue to do the physical, emotional, and spiritual work every single day. The way I see my body still isn't perfect, but it's worth fighting for. I love myself, and I accept myself at all stages and phases. I am beautiful simply because I am. As part of my personal healing and desire to help others, I have also become a certified Holistic Nutritionist and Registered Health Coach for people with

PCOS or anyone dealing with their own trauma bears surrounding food and their body. I've heard it said that broken people save broken people.

Should you encounter a bear, please try and remember the following:

IDENTIFY YOURSELF. There's nothing scarier to a bear than self-awareness. When you know yourself and can stand firm in your own beliefs, you no longer serve as prey. It takes a great deal of courage to explore your fear, your traumas, and your hurt. When you're ready to open up and bring them to light with the help of a trusted friend or professional, you'll begin to understand that you are more than your trauma and more than your pain.

PICK UP SMALL CHILDREN. Pick up your wounded or stunned inner child and get them off the ground to safety. This is not their battle to fight. Assure them that they are loved and protected by you. Take time to sit with your feelings, mourn your losses, and nurture yourself.

TRAVEL IN GROUPS. Find your people. Groups are intimidating to bears. Find people who are ready and willing to protect you or go to battle with you. When you feel that you're not enough, they will be your temporary strength and remind you of your own.

DO NOT ALLOW BEARS TO ACCESS YOUR FOOD. Your food is your fuel. Recognize patterns of shame and guilt, and recognize when food becomes a weapon or a shield. Tell a trusted friend and get professional help. Don't let the bears scare you away from your own nourishment.

DO NOT DROP YOUR PACK. Your pack is your backpack full of tools for your protection. This will also keep your back-end safe in case of an actual attack. Your pack is full of resources, truths, unwavering hope, and the courage to move forward.

Even if it doesn't seem like it now, you will survive. There may not be a $500,000 prize, but you are not alone.

You are enough.

You are worthy of true freedom from your bears.

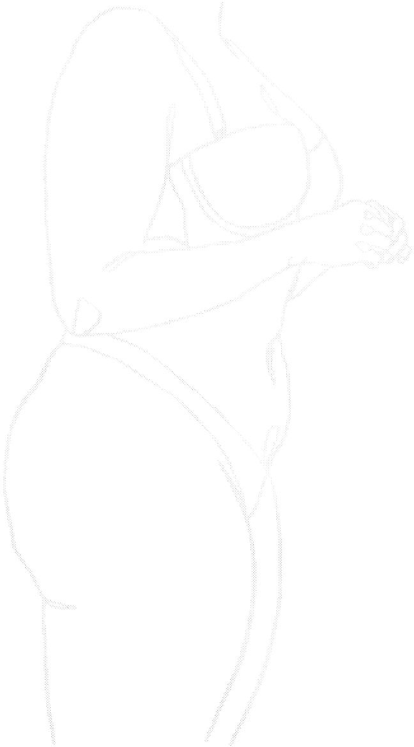

FORGIVING AND *releasing* PAST EMOTIONS, TRAUMA, ANGER, FEAR, AND RESENTMENT IS THE ONLY WAY TO RELEASE PAIN.

# Chapter 4

## ANGELA PHILLIPS

AUTHOR PHOTO: ALICIA THURSTON PHOTOGRAPHY
IG: @angiephillips37

As a child I could, just because I wanted to.

As a young adult I questioned if maybe I couldn't, but did because I had been able to before.

As a married woman I wondered if I couldn't, because others had expectations of me.

As a first-time mother I decided I shouldn't, because it should all be about her.

As a motherless daughter I couldn't even consider it, I was so filled with grief.

As a single woman I started to wonder again if I could, because maybe it was time.

As a solo parent I questioned whether I couldn't, because it was just me to provide for her.

As a new partner I questioned if I could, because it had been so long since I did.

As a mom to two I questioned how I could, because my time was owed to them.

One day I realized that if I didn't start to value myself – my needs, my wants, and my dreams – I couldn't show up for those around me. I couldn't honour the little girl that I was, the young woman I had been, the dark times when I felt I wasn't, and most importantly, the me I am now. Right now. Today.

My name is Angela. I am a daughter, a sister, an aunt, a mother, and a partner. I am a social worker, a lifelong learner, and I am passionate about helping others to move through trauma to wellness. I have experienced the loss of a parent, separation, and divorce, the world of dating a little later in life as a solo parent, the blending of my family, and adding another child to our mix.

I have placed my worth and my body on the back-burner for years and am working so hard to figure out who I am. I am still early on in this journey, but I am pretty proud of myself! I am humbled to be sharing my thoughts alongside so many other amazing women, and with you. We are so glad you are here.

When I was a little girl, my mother was diagnosed with Multiple Sclerosis, a chronic disease that affects the central nervous system. It impacted her vision, her mobility, and at times, her speech. I was so very aware of her body, how it might work one day and not the next. It meant that we might be able to go on an adventure one day, and not the next. It took us a little longer to get places, as we looked for ramps and curb cuts and accessible parking spots. I was also very aware of, and now am astonished by, how she used her abilities, her mind, her passion, and her grace to bless the world. She did not let herself become limited by what she could not do, and she did not let her body's deficits stop her from living life to the fullest.

My mom parented my sister and me in a way that encouraged us to be true to ourselves. She gave so much to those around her. It made me wonder at times, though, would my body fail me at some point? Would I stop being able to chase a ball and run around the neighbourhood with my friends? She didn't let her limitations stop her from doing good in the world, and I wanted to be just like her. I lost my mom well before I was ready, but I gained so much from her strength. As a child, I believed I could do anything because my mom showed me that I could. That child was so brave.

When I was a young woman, I looked at myself as an ongoing project – and with a little hard work, I obtained some obvious results. Between friends and daily tasks at home, I made time to do things that were good for me – things that made me happy. Through the years my focus shifted to who and what I would "be" when I finished school and started a career. If there was time I might stop at the gym or do an activity that I enjoyed outdoors, but as time went on there was always something else that needed to be done. I got caught up in what would be next and then next after that. I stopped doing things for me and always assumed there would be time later to focus on myself. I lost the sense of who I was, unless it related to who I was going to be.

When I became a married woman, I was young. Looking back, much too young. I worked tirelessly to set up a home, to work a job, to attend University. Each day seemed to be over before it began. I had a new name. I had a new role. I had a whole new family. All of a sudden I was responsible for grocery shopping, cooking, and cleaning. I was watching my bank account and paying bills. Occasionally I would look around to see who was in charge, who the adult was... only to realize it was me! I continued to lose myself, to cater to the needs of those around me, to make sure that they had everything they needed. I was slipping away.

When I became a first-time mom, I was overjoyed. This is what I had always wanted, a child. When I learned that I was pregnant, I knew that I had to do everything to make sure my daughter entered the world happy and healthy. I planned for months. I perfected her nursery. I made sure that she had all of the tiny clothes and shoes that she would need. I was going to be a mom, and I couldn't have been happier. When she arrived, I realized what it meant to love so much that you would do anything for them. She was my world, my whole entire world, and I let go of that final piece of me.

When I became a motherless daughter, I was lost. My mother, the woman who had been the force that held our family together, the one everyone called on to organize a gathering, to confirm a birthday or anniversary, or simply at the end of a long day for advice or accolades, was gone. A part of me, the person who knew me best, was no longer earthside. As we said goodbye, I had no idea what it would mean, really. But very quickly I realized that there was a hole in my heart, and I had no idea how to fill it. I went through each day hyper-focused on basic tasks and not much else. I did not eat well. I did not sleep well. I did not even consider reaching out for support. Weeks, months, and years seemed to pass in just a moment and dreadfully slowly all at once. I was without a safe space to land.

When I became a single woman, I was all of the sudden alone. I had given years to my marriage and now it had disappeared. I had no idea who I was without being half of a whole, for it had been that way for so long. I looked at myself in the mirror, literally, and did not recognize myself. I'd lay awake night after night, waiting for the garage door to open, waiting for the phone to ring, waiting to wake up and realize that it was a dream. Because if those things happened, then I would not need to figure out what was next for me. I would simply slip back into the day to day, and everything would be familiar again.

I questioned what I had done – and what I hadn't done – to end up in divorce. I wondered whether I was too much or too little, whether I was unlovable or undesirable. I felt myself slipping into darkness, into a place where there was immense sadness, anger, feelings of worthlessness, and shame. Those around me would comment on my strength, and commend me for getting through. I would smile and nod, and then return inward – to the darkness. I didn't like myself.

When I became a solo parent I questioned every one of my choices. I had a child to provide for, I had a house to maintain, I had a job to do. I questioned how I would keep up, and I felt guilty asking for help. As a mother to a daughter, I wanted to instill in her the very best qualities. I was reminded that everywhere I turned there were images, messages, and statements relating to what is good, what is right, and what is best. These messages made me fearful. In the past it had been fear that I was not enough, that my body was not right, that I was less than.

Then I became fearful of the images, messages, and statements that my child was exposed to. Everywhere my child turned, she could see products that reduced imperfections, ironed out lines and wrinkles, or food that made grand promises. She saw teenagers on social media purportedly living the perfect life in huge houses, with fancy cars and costly hobbies. I wanted her to love herself and those around her. I knew that I needed to instill in her what healthy relationships look like, what trust and respect look like, and I wondered how I could do this when she knew that her Dad and I had ended our marriage. I wanted her to be strong, successful, kind, and empathetic. And above all else, I wanted her to be happy. I couldn't let her down. I was so afraid.

When I became a partner to a new man, I was doubtful. I was doubtful that it would last. I was doubtful that I would be enough. I was doubtful that he would stay. I considered myself to be full of imperfections. After all, I was divorced, I had a child, and I did not have a perfect body. How could I expect someone else to take that on, to choose me? But days turned into months, and he didn't run. Months went by and he stayed. I started to wonder if this time it could be different.

When I became a mom of two, I considered my body to be like a machine. Producing two children a decade apart allowed me to consider the years between and how I had treated my body, a wonder capable of growing and nurturing actual humans. Did I provide it with enough fuel? Did it have enough time to reset? Did I service it enough? If I hadn't, would something happen to my baby? Was it already too late? Parenting during pregnancy meant that I couldn't always sleep when I needed to. Sometimes I ate on the run, or simply cleaned up a plate of crusts and discarded bites before we moved onto the next task. With my pregnancies came sickness the whole dang nine months. Was my baby getting what he needed from my body to grow healthy and strong and to arrive safely?

I have many people in my life who have taught me lessons aside from my mom. So many of them have imparted wisdom, shared family history or stories with me, encouraged me, supported me, and cared for me. Many of those people have also made me consider how I treat other people – how what I say impacts those around me, and how my comments (intentional and not so) make other people feel. It is amazing how something as simple as an intended compliment or small talk can have a negative impact on someone.

*"She's lost weight; she's looking good!"*

*"I haven't seen him in a while. I barely recognized him!"*

These examples may be seemingly harmless, but for the recipient or someone who overhears such a comment, the impact can be hurtful, harmful, and lasting. Does that mean she didn't look good before she lost weight? Does that mean you won't recognize him again if he gains some weight back?

One day I began to reflect on all my experiences in life and all of the roles that I have played: daughter, sister, mom, aunt, wife, and partner. There has been a lot of good and not-so-good that I have run, walked, and crawled through. In that moment, I considered that the constant in all of the light and dark places – was me. Me. Myself, my mind, and my body. My body… I am so thankful for my body.

Part of my journey has allowed me to consider what things I might have accomplished had I focused even a little bit on myself through all of the times of joy and those of sorrow, through childhood, my youth, during my time as a newly married woman, and then a mother. And then through losing my mom and my marriage, through darkness. Had I allowed myself some grace, some rest, and some hope, could I have done better or garnered the strength that I so desperately needed? If I had been more confident, could I have been more secure in my new relationship and more at ease as I moved through my pregnancy?

I have realized through much reflection that I cannot mourn what was, and I certainly cannot go back and change it, so I must live in a way going forward that honours the hard times, the losses and the grief. I must build myself up. I need to build myself to my full potential, for myself, first, and secondly for those around me. There will always be days when I question my worth and compare myself to someone else, but now instead of a sense of hopelessness and worthlessness, these moments will push me to re-frame my thoughts and promote kindness – just as much toward myself as those around me.

I am just at the beginning of the adventure, learning how to value my body and all that it does for me and my family each and every day. I am working so hard to remember to be present where my feet are, to be still, and to look around. I'm remembering to ask myself, *What will I make of today?* I have added myself to the list: groceries, check; laundry, check; homework help, check; honouring my body, check. And most importantly, I will reserve space for mistakes, for change, and for a lack of focus. On days that I struggle, I will no longer react with harshness, or with disappointment in myself. Rather, I will take the moment to reflect and choose to move forward with grace in all acts and love in every gesture… for tomorrow is another day to be ME.

# Chapter 5

## BRITTANY SCHMIDT

Author Photo: Alicia Thurston Photography
brittanyschmidt.ca | IG: @sprinkle.that.sparkle

### MY NAME IS BRITTANY SCHMIDT, AND I AM A BINGE-AHOLIC.

I'm fairly certain that's not even a word, but as of today you can add it to your dictionary. I am here to tell you a story about a little girl turned into an adult who has struggled with her self-image for most of her life. I know that I am not alone, and I hope that my chapter brings comfort to those who take the time to read it. Thank you for being here.

(I would love it if you would sing the next part of this bit in your head to the tune of *Fresh Prince of Bel Air*. Thanks.)

In Westvale suburbia, moved and raised
On the dirt hill is where I spent most of my days.

Chilling out relaxing, thought I was cool.

I used to play schlocky on the grounds of the school.

When a couple of guys that moved to my hood

Said a bunch of shit that didn't make me feel good.

I went through puberty and got awkward as hell
And learned to hate my body, from innocence I fell.

Thank you for playing along. I would really love to know how many people actually sang it with the tune in their head or maybe out loud.

Moving along.

Picture a girl in grade 6 who grew boobs long before most. They were little nubs; they did not require a sports bra or training bra, however many people around me started making comments about how I "should" wear a bra. The reason I put the word "should" in quotation marks is because it's a word that I absolutely despise… because it implies that we are missing the mark on something.

What started with comments about how I "should" cage the ladies quickly moved to comments about my choice of attire. I've never been one that really cared about dressing super fancy, and at this point in my life I was very put off by jeans. I refused to wear them because of the way they felt. This resulted in me prancing around in bright pink stirrup track pants.

As one can imagine, I became the butt of many jokes. Slap a pair of nubs on somebody dressed in bright pink stirrup pants and the comments about appearance came in fast and hot.

At the beginning I didn't let it bother me because I assumed that everyone got made fun of in some way, and I'm sure in some sense they did. After a few months it became bothersome and one of the first moments in my life when I remember being bullied for something appearance-related.

Fast-forward a few more years and I am in grade 9. I am sporting a short pixie haircut, glasses, and braces. You can imagine the ridicule that I experienced during that time frame. I was also one of those kids that would get super big when in a growth spurt, so there were times in my life when I would've been viewed as chubby, although it would quickly translate into growing taller, at least in the younger years.

When I turned 16, I met my first serious boyfriend and we decided that we were going to spend all of our money and time at Central Fresh Meat Market. We would often indulge in 2 L pop, chicken strips, and French fries. As you can imagine, by making choices like that, my body quickly ballooned. Coupled with the fact that I had increasing hormone changes, I sprinkled a little teenage chub onto my zits, glasses, braces, and short ass hair. #stunner

To put it lightly, it was the perfect clusterfuck for a storm of future body image issues.

Comments about my weight began floating around school and I gained a complex about the way I was feeling in my own skin. This was only the start of noticing how cruel people could be. It wasn't until I was fully out of high school and going to the bars that I noticed how their choice of words would impact me.

#squirrelmoment

I once was approached by a man who offered to buy me a drink. He came off super sleazy and I respectfully declined. His response was, "good, you're fat anyways!" To which I responded, "Why did you offer to buy me a drink in the first place then?"

Ummmmm duh… anywho, back to the story. #endsquirreling

I have always been extremely sensitive and although I now realize that it's my superpower, at that point in my life I was convinced that I was cursed!

Once I let go of some of the weight after this boyfriend and I parted ways, comments came in hard and fast yet again, but this time to my face. The interesting part about this is that you would assume that most of the comments would come when you are feeling terrible about yourself and being overweight; however, not many people said anything to my face at that point. I often heard about them through the grapevine/rumor mill. Who doesn't love knowing they are a topic of discussion when they're not around? #notme #sensitiveaf

I found it confusing that people would say derogatory things about my weight behind my back while I was struggling but took no issue commenting like crazy once I started, according to their standards, looking "good".

(Why did people feel the need to say anything at all?)

As I started to let go of more weight, people started to comment on how good I was looking and inside my mind I took that as a roundabout way of saying how much I looked like shit before.

Cue my start with becoming a binge eater.

I started to crave compliments from people. I wanted to be seen as somebody who had full control over her life. Somehow I equated that to controlling what I was eating so that I could maintain my look. I started to monitor what I was eating on a regular basis, which resulted in restricting what I would eat and later binging because I felt too restricted and just friggin' hungry.

I discovered on my healing journey that there was more to this binge eating mindset that was happening in my subconscious mind due to some trauma that I had endured over the course of my life. (But more on that later.)

I lived in the binge-and-restrict mindset for an extremely long time – so painfully long that it was very difficult to dig myself out of the mental hole that I had put myself in. I was so concerned about what other people thought of me and whether I was worthy of love. This terrible mindset that I got caught in slithered its way into so many areas of my life.

I would work out on a regular basis even though I hated it. I would deny myself treats at gatherings for the simple fact that somebody may be judging "the fat girl" for eating something unhealthy.

I had a mental catalog of all of the negative things that anybody had said to me in my past. Retrospectively, I gave them space in my mind and power over me that they didn't deserve.

I had gotten to a point where I tied my entire self-worth to the number on the scale. I would say the ultimate low for me was in my early 20s when I would let men treat me like shit for the simple fact that I didn't feel that I was worthy of love because I wasn't thin enough or good enough in some way.

FOR ANYBODY WHO IS READING THIS, I ASSURE YOU: NO MATTER WHAT YOUR RELATION TO GRAVITY IS, YOU ARE WORTHY OF BEING LOVED JUST FOR BEING YOU.

I struggled off and on throughout my 20s and things really came to a head when I turned 28.

Life seemed to be going swimmingly. I was engaged, about to be married, excited about my future, and had been eating extremely healthy and working out regularly to look my best in my dress.

I was so excited the day of my Buck and Doe on May 25th, 2013. This was a defining weekend in my life that I will never forget for as long as I live.

The day started with my fiancé and I heading out to some garage sales. We weren't going to see each other much that day until the party because of my hair and make-up trial, so we thought it would be fun to spend time together beforehand.

I had a gut feeling on the way home when we were driving past my parents' house to stop, so we did. It was 7:00 a.m. and there was no chance in hell that my parents were awake, but we stopped anyhow. They greeted us with open arms after the dog barking woke them, we kibbitzed (this is a word my mom often used which means joking around), and then had breakfast. It was an amazing few hours. I am so glad that I listened to my intuition.

Later that night at our Buck and Doe, my mom had a heart attack after feeling ill for a few hours. She had diarrhea and was vomiting at the end of the night and collapsed in the car as my parents left to head home.

PLEASE take note of how significantly different HEART ATTACKS present in women than men. If you know someone feeling unwell and is violently ill out of nowhere, do not fluff it off to "eating something that didn't agree with them." This is a sign of a heart attack and could be fatal. Things might have been different for my family had we recognized the signs, and had my mom allowed us to call the ambulance instead of assuming she had food poisoning.

The end of our Buck and Doe was horrifying. I remember as my mom and dad walked down the stairs I peered over the ledge and shouted, "Mom, I love you, call me when you get home" with the worst feeling in my stomach that I would never speak to her again. I just knew. Another life lesson from the Britt Schmidt show: ALWAYS, and I mean ALWAYS, listen to your INTUITION. It will never steer you wrong.

A few minutes after they left, my dad came flying up the stairs while I was talking to a friend about how worried I was for my mom. He said she had a stroke in the car in the parking lot as they were about to leave; his face told another story. I ran past him and down the stairs faster than a lightning bolt to find my mom in the back of an ambulance being resuscitated by the EMTs.

I held my father-in-law's hand the entire way to the hospital as he drove us. My mind was spinning. I went from joking and laughing with my friends to completely sober and terrified yet calm in a matter of moments. It was a very strange headspace as we trailed behind the ambulance.

We stayed at the hospital until she was out of surgery around 7:00 a.m. the next morning, when the doctor came into the waiting room and told us to go home. Her body was on ice to keep the swelling down and the stints had been inserted.

We went home to catch a few hours' sleep. I woke up suddenly around 10:30 a.m. to pick up the phone to call my dad, while he was already calling me… she was gone.

All her ribs were broken, causing internal bleeding, which happens when someone has CPR performed on them. She had osteoporosis and was a heavy smoker for many years. All the odds had been stacked against my sweet mom.

When we got to the hospital, I flung myself at the nurse as she confirmed that my mom had passed. I cried in her arms for a very long time. Little did I know that later in life, I would be helping this same nurse with the transition of two losses within her family by selling their homes. Everything comes full circle, and I am thankful for the comfort this beautiful soul gave me.

My mom was my best friend. We used to sing, dance, laugh, cry, and talk all the time. Every weekday we would call each other at 4:20 p.m. because we would both be off work. Many times, I would pick up the phone and she'd already be on the line, and we would giggle at how in tune we were with one another, chat about the day, and make plans to hang out.

She had a way of making those around her feel as if they'd known her their whole life. You'd tell her your entire story in a short time of being in her energy because you felt so comfortable and safe. She was magical; you'd come to her with a problem, she'd acknowledge your feelings and redirect your way of thinking about the problem into something productive while making you feel seen and heard.

I am so grateful for having such a positive influence in my life and a loving relationship with my mom. I am extremely fortunate.

After she passed away, I felt lost. Especially with my body image. I had lost a significant amount of weight due to her passing and dealing with the waves of grief.

I am bawling as I write this and continue to work through what I've experienced. It's been eight-and-a-half years – and it still feels so raw. Grief is not linear, and if you are going through something similar, know that there is no "right" way to grieve, only the way that feels aligned for you. I decided early on not to let others determine how I do it; it's not their burden to bear.

I had my first baby 11 months afterward, and I was able to "bounce back" to my pre-baby weight within six months. You would've thought that I deserved a Nobel Prize for how I carried on and how many people I told about the weight loss because I was so proud that I was able to get back to this weight. What a ridiculous thought at this point in my life when I am in so much of a better place regarding my body. I wish that the beautiful 29-year-old version of myself would've spent more time being proud of herself for how she was navigating motherhood and grief and less time caring about what other people thought about her weight.

Denying my body nutrition and fuel during a time frame when I was so vulnerable to postpartum depression and struggling with lack of sleep while managing it all – was probably one of the worst things that I could've done for myself. As usual, hindsight is 20/20.

On my first born's first birthday, we got pregnant with our second child. I remember being so excited about the thought of the second baby and then the second thought that I had was immediately about how this would impact my body. Saying it out loud, I feel about as shallow as a puddle.

*I want to pause there for a second. I want to acknowledge and congratulate myself and anybody else that is reading this book on how far you've come. Writing this book has been one of the most amazingly vulnerable growth opportunities that I have ever experienced. I was forced to revisit many parts of my story that I thought I had closed, which brought to the surface many tears and resulted in a further level of healing. Thank you, Andrea and Courtney, for coming up with this idea of Body Bliss. I am proud to be here.*

Back to the puddle. #squirreled

When I think back to the version of myself who was 30 years old and pregnant again, I think of a woman who spent many hours and brain space thinking about what she was going to eat and not following her intuition when it came to food. I would come into conversations and make excuses for myself as to why I was as big as I was or what I was doing to lose weight and workout because I felt judged.

Another revelation of Brittany Schmidt: nobody cares how much you weigh as much as you do, unless you're a boxer.

The biggest struggle that I had with my second pregnancy was going to my OB/GYN and having them repeatedly tell me that I was tracking overweight and that I needed to stop eating junk food, and basically just making me feel like a big bag of shit. I struggled with nausea like nothing you've ever seen and felt sick for the entire duration of both pregnancies.

At the time I had a toddler at home who had chronic ear infections and I was spending a lot of time with an Ear, Nose, and Throat Specialist begging them to allow her to get tubes put in and remove adenoids and tonsils. The last thing that I needed to hear at the time was basically that I was becoming a porker and that I needed to get a handle on my eating. Banana nut muffins from Tim Horton's were the only things that I could keep down without wanting to throw up on the side of the road like I had just drank 10 shots and had the night of my life.

I will never forget sitting in the waiting room wanting to hear the update on my baby and instead being told that I needed to slow down on the eating.

*ARE YOU KIDDING?*

Cue a heavy restriction for the next few weeks while I sorted out the feeling of judgment that I walked away with.

I gave birth to my second beautiful baby all naturally without any drugs and I felt like superwoman. Just like my first daughter, I was surrounded by so much love, and these sweet girls were counting on me to provide them with sustenance, love, and support. All of the judgment that I had felt over the years melted away – for a little while.

There's something about just having a baby where people seem to give you a little more leeway in how they view your body – and honestly, I gave myself a bit more as well.

After C was born, I ended up with what I think was undiagnosed postpartum depression and I was really struggling to be in the house. Both of my girls had lip ties and tongue ties and nursing was extremely painful. Sidebar: you don't win a prize for suffering through horrific breastfeeding issues. I received ZERO gold stars for what I endured.

About six months in, I decided to formula feed and that I would go back to work early. My husband would take a three-month paternity leave. I was so excited to go back at first, but I quickly remembered why I struggled there. I constantly felt judged walking down the halls with people giving me the up-and-down. I had gone back to work significantly heavier than when I started, and this behavior was triggering for me.

I even had a few people, including my family, ask while I was pregnant with both girls whether or not I was having twins, or afterward, whether I was pregnant again.

Those people got blocked from any social media because that is just an intolerable thing to say to anyone and I will not enable the behavior by allowing inconsiderate people like that to have access to me. #boundaries

During this time frame I continued to restrict and binge and restrict and binge.

Here's the thing: If you restrict long enough, you start to see results, and at one point I was able to let go of a very significant amount of weight... and again the comments about how good I was looking started up.

I do realize that many people make these comments with the intention of giving you positive reinforcement. What they don't realize is that somebody like myself who has struggled so hard for so long would view it as a trigger, and not as a compliment. I wonder how many people feel the same way.

Soon into my return to work, I toyed with the idea of letting go of my corporate life and pursuing real estate, which is where my true passion lies. This went on for seven full months while I studied in my spare time, got licensed, and sold my first house.

I finally decided to leave the corporate world.

In the end I left for a mixture of the following reasons:

- I was no longer able to help people in my own way.
- I never felt like I fit in.
- I constantly felt judged.
- I was told that I had basically hit my maximum income level without formally going to University.

I didn't see the value in attending university for something that I wasn't extremely passionate about. So at that point, between losing my mom and realizing that time is very limited on this earth, and the fact that I wanted to pursue something that I was very passionate about, (helping people) – I decided to cut ties.

It was 2018 when I finally left, and I felt like a huge weight had been lifted off my shoulders and my physical body.

I had completely underestimated the physical toll that working this job was taking on me. I quickly realized that by not being in fight or flight mode on a daily basis, my body shed 15 pounds of unwanted weight. I had never been happier, and I was so excited to go out on my own and make a name for myself in the real estate world, which is exactly what I spent the next three years doing.

All the while, I continued to binge and restrict and binge and restrict. I would go out for lunches with people, eat way too much food, and then I would not eat for an entire 12 hours to make sure that I had a caloric deficit to meet my requirements for Weight Watchers or MyFitnessPal or whatever tool it was that I was using to hold myself accountable. This mindfuck that I endured began to take its toll on my mental health. I had spent so much time and energy worrying about what I ate, worrying about what other people thought of me, and judging myself. I got to the point where I was allowing my lack of self-confidence to dictate what I would or wouldn't do.

I stopped swimming with my girls in pools if there were a lot of people around. I didn't want to be seen. I kept the same crappy headshot for three years because I looked skinny in it. I was not doing the fun real estate videos that I wanted to do because I was afraid of how people would react to me living my authentic truth.

I held onto a lot of shame from others' comments about me over the years, I gave people power who didn't deserve it, and I took away the power that I should've been giving to fully show up as my highest self.

I often felt so sad and defeated about my body image and how OBSESSED I was about food that it became counterintuitive.

Anyone who knows me knows that sadness and defeat are not mindsets that I am comfortable staying in.

Cue the Covid-19 pandemic in 2020.

I was still trucking along doing my binge and restrict song and dance and BOOM! I was blindsided like everyone else in the world by COVID!

Since Mom passed, I have been on what you could call a spiritual awakening. I've always known that I was an empathic intuitive, and up until this point, I had generally ignored a lot of the signs. I have always been connected to and loved nature. I thought I could control the weather as a kid. Songs would come on the radio when I was thinking of something directly related to them. I see repetitive angel numbers, birds all the time, ringing ears, and words that directly relate to my thoughts randomly out in public. A heron would fly past the window in my basement office daily, and somehow I would manage to see it every single day. I could probably spend an entire week just talking about anything intuition and empathic related, but I digress.

Boom goes the dynamite! We're in the middle of a pandemic. I am lying in bed one night, and I get an intuitive hit that I need to start yoga. A few people have mentioned it to me often throughout the course of my life, and for whatever reason up until now I've ignored it.

I go on Google and come across a wonderful woman called Adriene who runs a free website via YouTube called *Yoga with Adriene*. I felt an instant connection with this stranger who is so down-to-earth and makes you feel absolutely welcome in your own skin. She creates a space where you feel confident being who you are on the mat – and in your life. She takes things slow and easy and creates different modifications for those whose bodies don't fit in the shapes she's teaching. Her language is inclusive and not body, shape, size, or ability-focused. I felt so safe that I started doing yoga every day. What I didn't realize at the time was that yoga was slowly but surely realigning my nervous system to go from a place of fight or flight to a place of calm.

It was perfect divine timing, and I couldn't be more thankful for discovering the benefits of yoga. Having two little kids at home while you're trying to do online learning, as many readers know, is a complete Schmidt show. I have a story about how I made a debut in one of my daughters' classes on Zoom while on the toilet, but that's a story for another time. #squirreledagain

I decided that it was time to do something about my eating habits. I couldn't put my finger on exactly what it was that I was struggling so hard with. I had a friend who was in therapy, and she has a similar binge eating habit. Her therapist suggested something to her called intuitive eating and asked her, "what is the weight protecting you from?"

This question hit me like a SCHMIDT TON OF BRICKS.

What was this weight protecting me from?

Around this time, I was also doing a manifestation course that talks a lot about the subconscious mind and how it impacts our conscious mind and reality.

After a few deep dives sorting myself out and navigating limiting beliefs that were stuck in my subconscious mind and intuitive hits/messages, I realized that one of the reasons that I was overeating was as a form of protection.

*[TRIGGER WARNING – Sexual Assault]*

FOR ANYBODY WHO IS READING THIS, I ASSURE YOU: NO MATTER WHAT YOUR RELATION TO GRAVITY IS, YOU ARE WORTHY OF BEING LOVED JUST FOR BEING *you.*

A few times throughout the course of my life I have been sexually assaulted by strangers or acquaintances. Each time this happened, it was during a time when I was feeling thin and seen. Cat calls, inappropriate comments about my appearance, grabbing at bars, people assuming my friendly nature is an invitation when it is NOT.

Part of my binge eating is to protect myself from being seen and potentially assaulted again.

It CLICKED. This was one of many reasons that I had been struggling so hard with this horrible habit, disease, or whatever you want to call it.

It was time to change, but how?

One morning I was lying in bed again, my mind was completely clear, and out of nowhere I got another intuitive hit that said, "stop tracking what you eat." This felt like one of the most prolific moments in my life. I could feel that it was a turning point for me. I got up and I walked out into the living room, turned to my husband and said, "FUCK THIS SHIT."

Naturally my husband had no idea what the hell I was talking about, and I'm fairly certain that he thought I was off my rocker. I sat down and explained to him all that's happened that I blocked out, and how I was sitting in bed this morning thinking about all of the time and energy that I had put into restricting and binging what I was eating. I was very ashamed and embarrassed by how detrimental that was to my mental health and my body. I had been protecting myself and I was going to need to find new ways to protect myself from feeling like it's unsafe to be seen.

I spent a lot of time crying and forgiving myself for feeling like I was unable to be who I am and undeserving of a fit body for fear that someone may take an interest in it.

I am proud to say that I am no longer afraid of being seen, in any light. I do my crazy real estate videos because it's fun and makes me feel good. Do I get negative comments? Sure. Do they bother me? Sometimes. Do I do it anyway? HELL YEAH.

Do I show up as the best mother and wife that I am capable of? YES, to the best of my capacity at the time.

Am I afraid of the potential of being physically harmed again? Sometimes; however, if anyone makes a comment about my looks the conversation is immediately shut down and I give myself a STRONG and CONFIDENT voice to ensure that whoever I am with knows that they are barking up the wrong tree. I also took a few self-defense courses to increase confidence so I feel that I can protect myself if needed.

Somewhere along the way I lost sight of the courageous, beautiful, fearless, bold, funny, outgoing, excitable, fun, and caring version of myself. I am slowly finding my way back to her with a few daily rituals that I want to share with you all, as they may benefit your inner child as well.

I start my day with yoga, intention-infused water, affirmations, and sometimes journaling.

My affirmations sound something like this:

*It is safe for me to be seen and heard.*
*I am worthy of a fit body.*
*I eat intuitively and fuel my beautiful body with healthy foods.*
*I am forever, and in all ways, enough.*
*I show up on hard days.*

I believe in affirmations and journaling prompts so much that I am creating a card deck that can be used as affirmations and flipped to the back with deep dive questions. They will act as journal prompts to help others to get to know themselves intimately and move into a positive and productive mindset. You can also take the deck to parties to use to get to know your friends in a new way.

I have always wanted to connect with others on a deeper level. I feel that these cards will help people to sort through challenges, provide guidance, and get to know themselves better while creating a deeper connection to yourself and others (should you choose to work through the deck in small groups). I cannot wait to release them to the world via my Instagram @ sprinkle.that.sparkle, my website, and Amazon!

Here's the thing: despite all of the work that I have done and the ways that I have changed, I am not perfect and I still catch myself having intrusive thoughts regarding my body. The difference now is that I acknowledge how I am feeling, wish those feelings well, and flip the script to something positive about myself. It doesn't always work, but when it does, I am left feeling so much better!

Which brings me to one final thought before I bid you adieu.

Whenever I am feeling low about whatever it is I am going through, there is one thing that my dad taught me when I was very young that has proven effective NO MATTER WHAT.

If he noticed that I was sad because of bullies, struggles, challenges, etc. that I was facing, he would have me sit in front of the mirror as I stared at myself and say, "WHO ARE YOU?" and I would respond, making eye contact with myself and yelling, "I am BRITTANY LYNN SCHMEARER!!!!!" as loud as I possibly could and as many times as it took until I felt confident facing my challenge.

I still use it to this day with my new last name and with my two beautiful baby girls.

They are a couple of the major reasons that I will fight daily to provide a good example of positive self-love. I want them to understand that they are their own best friend and advocate in this life, and that accepting and loving yourself is extremely important.

So, I'll leave you with this: the next time you're feeling low, settle in front of the mirror, lock eyes with yourself and ask the question, "WHO ARE YOU?"

YELL your reply," I AM _______ ________!!!" as many times as it takes to feel like you can take on the world.

Lean into how empowered it makes you feel, because you, my friend, are (insert your awesome name here) and you are a force. Never forget that!

. I *believed* THAT MY EXCESS WEIGHT WAS THE CAUSE OF MY UNHAPPINESS, WHEN IN FACT, IT WAS THE OTHER WAY AROUND.

# Chapter 6

# ERIN ELLA ZARZECZNY

Author Photo: Alicia Thurston Photography
IG: @erinellacoaching

Do you know what it's like to despise your body?

Do you know how it feels to be disgusted by what you see in the mirror?

Well, I do. I know because I have been there. I know the challenges that many women face when it comes to loving their bodies because I have been in the depths of self-hate and self-loathing. After struggling with this for most of my life, I have found my way out. It might sound simple, but my journey has been anything but easy. It has taken a ton of hard work to get to where I am today. Although I am now "on the other side," my journey to self-acceptance and to loving my body is exactly that. It is a journey. There is no destination and the road is not straight. I have had so many ups and downs along the way. There were moments and periods of darkness when I hated my body so much that it seemed impossible that I would ever be able to love myself. There have also been better days of growth, joy, and happiness.

Loving myself and my body is a choice that I make every day. It is a commitment that I made to myself for the long run. It's a journey that doesn't end. My name is Erin and I am a fun-loving mom of two, and today, as a women's empowerment coach, I help women take back their power and learn to love themselves and their bodies – whatever the number on the scale. I tell my story today so that women like you, who may be struggling like I was and may be in their darkest moments, know that they are not alone and that even though it might not seem possible, it will get better. If it did for me, it can for you.

It is widely accepted that our experiences in childhood have a profound and lasting impact on our lives and shape who we are. My journey with my body started when I was six. I started gymnastics at a young age and I loved it from the beginning. I loved being at the gym. It was like a playground for me. I loved swinging on the high bars and running and tumbling into the foam pit. I enjoyed jumping on the trampoline and flipping high in the air. I started competing shortly after and my love for tumbling and flipping became more serious. By the age of eight, I was training for 20 hours a week. Competing at the provincial level was no joke. I was put on a modified schedule at school so that I could train. I would go to school in the morning and leave in the afternoon so that I could be at the gym. Gymnastics was my life.

If you don't know anything about gymnastics, I will tell you the key to being a top athlete in this sport. The goal of gymnastics is to get as close to a perfect score as you can. You are judged individually on your performance, and then ranked among your competitors based on your score. The more perfect your performance, the better. This is what you strive for as a gymnast; perfection. Perfection became my motivator. I would practice the same move literally hundreds of times, each time getting closer and closer to perfect. As I grew up in this sport, I started to show perfectionist tendencies outside of the gym as well. My hair always had to be perfectly done, with not one piece out of place. School projects took me hours to complete, making sure that they were "just right."

There are a lot of great things about the sport of gymnastics, many of which I experienced firsthand. I met some incredible people during my time, many of whom I am still friends with to this day. The pressure to be perfect, however, was a heavy weight to bear.

Over the next few years, I stopped performing as well in competitions. I developed what my sports therapist at the time called "mental blocks," in which I was unable to perform a move that I had done hundreds of times before. I felt that I wasn't good enough, and was embarrassed about my inability to perform. I thought for sure that there must be something wrong with me!

I left the sport of gymnastics when I was 12. It was the hardest, heaviest decision that I had ever made, and for my 12-year-old self, this was a lot to handle. I felt so much shame around quitting. I truly believed that I was a failure. In the six short years that I was in the sport, I internalized some limiting beliefs that would follow me throughout my life.

Although I was no longer in gymnastics, I carried the quest to be perfect into my teen years – except now I wanted to have the perfect body. At the age of 13, I was considered short compared to my peers of the same age. At 5 feet 2 inches tall, I would have done anything to be 5 foot 8. Not only was I not tall, but I had an athletic build. I would look at myself in the mirror and what I saw was less than the ideal body type – and I hated it.

I refused to wear jeans because they made my thighs look fat. I picked apart every single inch of my body, compared myself to other girls in my class, and felt that I didn't measure up. I became so self-conscious and lacked confidence. I didn't believe that I was beautiful or pretty, and all I could see were my flaws. Looking back, I see how I began to connect my negative beliefs about my "imperfect" body with my self-worth. It started as feelings of inadequacy, and over time, turned into deep rooted self-hate. I internalized these feelings and beliefs and waged war on my body.

Throughout highschool I looked primarily outside of myself for validation. Those were hard years and the struggle to accept myself continued. I went away to University at the age of 18. Between the cafeteria food, the partying, and the lack of exercise, I gained 20 pounds in my first year. This is pretty typical for anyone who goes away to University, but as someone who entered with already low self-esteem, this gutted me. I knew that I wanted to be in shape and feel good, but I didn't, and my confidence plummeted even further. I really didn't know what it meant to take care of my body – to nourish it properly, to get enough rest, and to move it regularly.

In addition to not knowing how to care for myself physically, I also didn't know how to properly handle my emotions. As a way of coping with my feelings of social isolation, low self-worth, and lack of direction in life, I started to binge eat candy and junk food. I would eat until I felt sick. Then I would feel guilt and shame, which would only land me back at the cupboard for more chocolate. Food became my way of dealing with hard feelings and emotions that I didn't know how else to process. Eating junk food also gave me a momentary escape from the reality that I was otherwise living. I had zero self-esteem, zero confidence, and zero self-worth. I felt so bad about myself that I didn't go out most days, which made it hard to make friends. Even when I did go out, I had no idea how to be myself or how to have fun. These were supposed to be the best years of my life, and it felt anything but.

Building connections was not the only thing that I was missing out on. My issues with my body and my low self-esteem impacted all aspects of my life. One summer between semesters at University, I was with my mom and sister in Florida. One night, we had plans to go out for dinner, but I was feeling so insecure about my body that I couldn't leave my hotel room. I sat and sobbed because I couldn't find anything to wear that I felt good in. I desperately wanted to feel beautiful, but what I saw instead were my fat thighs, wide hips, and excess weight around my stomach. My mom and sister pried me off the hotel room floor, telling me over and over again how beautiful I was. I eventually made it out for dinner, but their platitudes fell on deaf ears.

This scenario was not the first or the last of its kind. There were more times than I can count where my night started and ended with me crying alone and feeling utterly hopeless and defeated. I simply was unable to see my beauty, my uniqueness, or my worth. I constantly had thoughts that I would never be pretty enough or tall enough or skinny enough.

I refer to this period of my life as "the dark days." It was lonely and I so desperately wanted things to be different. I wanted to be able to get dressed and feel good about myself. I wanted to exude confidence. Mostly, I wanted to live my life without the heaviness of my insecurities. I just couldn't see past my imperfections. It felt like heavy chains were tied to my feet. I didn't know how I was ever going to break free.

I wish my story got better from there, but it didn't. I made it through University, but my struggle to love my body continued. I continued to use food as a way of coping. I would eat when I was feeling bored, anxious, sad, and for reasons other than hunger. I would also binge eat, meaning that I would eat an enormous amount of food in one sitting, and felt unable to stop. It was typical for me to eat a bag of chips, an entire box of cookies, chocolate, and candy in one sitting. My binge would sometimes last for hours. It was almost as if I was in a trance, an unconscious state. I would zone out and then a couple of hours later, I would come back to my body and realize what I had eaten. I would be so full and completely disgusted with myself.

I would make a promise to myself that I would never do it again – however this pattern was addicting.

Even though I knew how I would feel after, I would still do it. I craved that hit of feel-good chemicals that sugar would send to my brain. I also craved the temporary dissociation that happened so that I could escape the unhappiness and dissatisfaction that I was feeling in my life.

I tried everything to stop the cycle of binge eating. I would meal prep and only buy the food necessary for what I was making. I would go for walks during the evenings, which is when I would typically binge eat. Nothing worked. Inevitably, I would find myself back at the closest grocery store with a cart full of goodies. Many times I would call my mom in tears after a binge and would cry and scream for help in stopping this cycle. My mom always took my call with care and compassion and with some new strategies to try. Anyone who knows what binge eating is like will know that it's not easy to stop. Binge, shame, binge some more, self-hate and shame, binge again. I continued to eat this way for the next five years of my life. I felt lost, alone, hopeless, and unhappy.

I blamed my unhappiness on my inability to stop the binge eating cycle. I thought that I was unhappy because of the extra weight I was carrying due to my overeating. I was convinced that if I could just stop binge eating and lose weight, all of my problems would be solved. I exercised every day to try to shed the weight, but no matter how intense or how long my workouts were, the number on the scale didn't budge. I tried every diet in the book hoping that the latest trendy diet would be the one that broke my binge eating pattern and turned my life around. If I could just lose weight, I would be happier, find my dream job, and be in a loving relationship. **I believed that my excess weight was the cause of my unhappiness, when in fact, it was the other way around.**

At this point in my life, I had little-to-no self-worth. I was well into my 20s and was completely disconnected from my true self. The decisions that I made reflected this, and I entered into a romantic relationship that continued to break me down. I didn't respect or love myself, so how could I expect someone else to? Over the next five years, I put an incredible amount of effort into making this relationship work. Even though I saw the red flags, I refused to believe that my relationship was doomed. Since unconsciously I did not believe that I was worthy of respect, fulfillment, or love, I put up with emotional abuse and disrespect.

The worst part was that I wasn't the one who finally ended the relationship. I would have continued to try and make it work at all costs, but he was the one who ended things. Talk about kicking me when I was down. This was more evidence that I wasn't loveable or worthy.

When things ended, I was a complete mess. I spent days in bed crying, feeling hopeless, and depressed. I felt like I had hit rock bottom. I sobbed thinking of all of the years that I spent hating my body, struggling with binge eating, and being disrespected by men. I didn't know who I was anymore, and maybe I never did. Deep down I knew that something had to change for good. I simply couldn't continue this way. This wasn't how I wanted to live my life. I knew that I was strong and that I would come out the other side, but I had no idea how I was going to do it. So I did what I knew I had to, and put one foot in front of the other. I slowly started to rebuild myself, one brick at a time.

There was not one event or "aha" moment that caused me to see myself or my body differently. If you are reading this and are in the depths of emotional eating, self-hate, body dysmorphia, or a toxic relationship, hearing that there is no magic pill to make it better can be hard. I know this because I prayed for a magic pill to take all of the pain and hurt away. I prayed for happiness and confidence and to finally BE FREE. I truly believe that I had to go through all of my struggles to find out what it means to love myself. At the core of all of my experiences growing up was a lack of self-love and self-worth.

Progress didn't happen overnight. It was a slow climb, but over time and with a lot of work, I was able to find self-acceptance, own my worth, and find my version of body bliss. I want to share with you the things that helped me and the lessons that I've learned along the way in the hopes that it will help you, wherever you are on your journey.

## OWN YOUR POWER.

The shifts and changes that ensued after the end of my toxic relationship put my life on a completely different trajectory. The change in direction came from the decision that I made to take control of my life and to start making choices that were right for ME. From that point forward, every decision that I made, big or small, I chose to do what I needed to do to feel good. In doing this, I took back the keys to my own car and got in the driver's seat. In other words, I took back my power. These decisions included: moving into a new condo that had more space and was in a part of town that I loved, building back my other relationships and friendships that I had been ignoring over the years, putting boundaries in place, and setting standards for how I wanted to be treated and how I would treat myself. As a result of all of these choices, I began to feel better about myself and I stopped turning to food as an escape. I started to binge eat less and less.

I want to reiterate that this did not happen overnight. I continued to stumble along the way, but for the first time in a long time I felt empowered, and I began to open up to the possibility of happiness. I could not have predicted the changes that would occur when I stopped trying to please others, when I stopped hiding, and when I stopped letting my insecurities run my life.

With change and growth comes new perspectives, new opportunities, and more possibilities. As it would turn out, I met someone about a year later who, to this day, respects me and supports me unconditionally. If you are struggling with low self-worth, start making choices that feel empowering for you – because even a small shift can completely change the direction that your ship is heading and can bring about events that you could never have imagined. Once I started making decisions that felt good for ME, everything else started to fall into place.

## NOURISH YOUR SOUL.

As I began to put myself first, I discovered that there were things that nourished me on a deeper level. What I learned through my struggle with binge eating is that I was eating to fill a void. I felt empty inside. I wasn't being fulfilled by my job or my partner at the time, and I certainly wasn't giving any love to myself. I also lacked direction in life. To fill these feelings of emptiness and general unhappiness, I ate. When I started to fill my life with things that I loved and when I made career and relationship choices that felt aligned and good, I stopped binge eating as much. It was really important for me to find things that filled me up other than food. I started to fill my life with people, hobbies and jobs that made me feel good and that I loved. For me this was a game changer. I had ignored my soul's desires for so long that at first I didn't even know where to begin. Once I started to connect to myself and listen to my intuition, I found what I was really craving… and it wasn't food. It was all the things that nourished my soul.

What I also learned is that my binge eating and subsequent weight gain was a symptom of my unhappiness; it was not the cause. I was unhappy in other areas of my life and binge eating was how I dealt with it. The struggle that

I was experiencing with my eating habits was a message telling me that I needed to make changes in my life – except it took me years to decode this message and stand in my power to make those changes.

If you are feeling stuck in your unhappiness, get to the source. Inquire and listen to your inner voice. It might be tempting to fill the void or to numb your uncomfortable emotions with food, shopping, drinking, etc., but you will only be keeping yourself where you are. When you find things that you love and that fill you up on a deeper level, you will feel less inclined to engage in destructive behaviors. You are never stuck, you always have a choice, and above all, you are worthy of the kind of happiness that knocks your socks off.

## LISTEN TO YOUR BODY.

Another part of my journey was deciding that I deserved to feel good in my body, to have energy, and to take care of myself. Breaking the cycle of binge eating and the poor habits that accompanied it was difficult. Even though I decided that it was time to heal my relationship with food, I continued to have bad days where the power of my habits were incredibly strong and I ended up binge eating. Over time, however, the number of good days every week started to outweigh the number of bad days. What helped in tipping the scale was listening to my body. I started to notice the foods that made me feel good and the foods that didn't. I began to view food as nourishment rather than an escape. I wanted to feel alive, energetic, and strong, and so the majority of the time, I ate foods that made me feel that way.

Today I continue to listen to what my body tells me, and I am able to stop eating when I am full. I can have a few cookies and close the bag instead of continuing to eat until it's empty. Dieting never worked for me, and it was not the way that I found self-acceptance. What I do believe in is intuitive eating, which is about listening to your body and responding by giving it what it needs. I no longer restrict certain foods or think of food as either "good" or "bad." I eat what my body craves and what gives me the most energy. And yes, some days it's pizza and french fries, and other days it's a beautiful salad.

I also listen to my body when it comes to exercise. I exercise to feel good, not as punishment for what I ate the day before. I move my body because I desire to be strong and to feel my best. I let my body tell me what type of movement feels good that day. I also listen to my body when it tells me

THERE WILL BE TIMES
WHEN I AM SKINNIER AND
TIMES WHEN I AM A FEW
POUNDS HEAVIER. THIS DOES
NOT DEFINE MY *worth.*

I need to rest, and I don't beat myself up for taking a couple of days off. I am in this for the long run, and I prioritize my health and my wellness. Some days that means foregoing exercise for time with family and friends. Although there was no magic pill that changed things around for me, I do know that as I focused less on attaining the perfect body and more on feeling good and being happy, the more weight I let go of, and the more comfortable I felt in my body.

## FORGIVE YOURSELF.

What kept me in the cycle of binge eating for so many years were the feelings of shame and guilt that inevitably followed a binge. Shame and guilt not only fuelled my self-hate, they also perpetuated the cycle. These low-vibe emotions made me feel horrible. Shame and guilt are vicious and halt any chance of moving forward. When I started to show myself more kindness and compassion after a binge, a subsequent binge became less likely. When I didn't make myself feel shitty for binge eating, I was less likely to do it again. I started to investigate some of the things that would trigger a binge and became an observer of my behavior. I stopped calling myself names and looking at myself with disgust. I don't want to oversimplify this, because believe me, it was hard to show myself love when I fell off track and dipped back into old patterns. It took countless tries and many failed attempts, but eventually I stopped punishing myself with harsh words and self-defeating behaviors. Forgiving myself was the key.

I also want to highlight the importance of seeking and receiving support along my healing journey. I would not be "on the other side" if it wasn't for the support that I had throughout. My family was pivotal in helping me get through my dark days. I am very fortunate that I have always had an extremely supportive family unit. I didn't even have to ask, and they were there for me. I know that this is not necessarily the case for everyone, so if you don't have readily available support among family or friends, seek support elsewhere. Support groups, women's circles, female empowerment tribes – whatever it may be – seek it without shame and take it if it is there.

## LOVE YOUR BODY IN EVERY SEASON.

I got pregnant with my son when I was 31, and with my daughter when I was 33. As with all pregnancies and babies, the course of my life changed forever. With each pregnancy, my body changed, and so the work that I had been doing to heal my relationship with myself and my body was put to the test. Weight fluctuations, cravings, pre- and post-birth acne, and sagging skin became my new reality.

I decided during and after my pregnancies to be more compassionate toward myself and my body. It was time to let go of the quest for perfection and drop unrealistic expectations. I began to accept my body as it was, because of what it was: an incredible vessel, the home to my soul, the vehicle that pushed out a baby! Even in the sleepless nights and crying babies, I chose to put myself first. I continued to prioritize my self-care and believed that I was the best mom when I was feeling good. Going through pregnancy and childbirth helped me to see that as women, our bodies go through seasons during our lifetime.

**There will be times when I am skinnier and times when I am a few pounds heavier. This does not define my worth.** At the same time, it is important – in fact, it is imperative – to take care of my body in every season. I take care of it with good food, sleep, movement, connection, and positive self-talk. It is no longer about being a certain size or weight, fitting into society's mold, or another person's expectations of how I should look. It is about caring for the physical vessel that houses my dreams and desires. It is about feeling good and having enough energy to do the things that I love to do – playing with my kids, going for walks with my husband, or going out to dinner with friends. For so many years I was so consumed and focused on my weight and how I looked, that I was missing out on life. Now I take care of my body. I no longer give my power away to the way that I look. I know that I am the most powerful when I am taking care of my body.

## PERFECTION IS UNATTAINABLE.

I know this may sound cliché, but there is no such thing as perfect. I spent so many years of my life hating my body and the way I looked. I thought that once I had the perfect body, I would be worthy of living my life and experiencing joy and happiness. What actually happened was that my issues with my body stopped me from experiencing life. My quest for perfection caused me to miss out on events and experiences and fun times with family and friends that I will never get back. I lost myself during my dark days, but what I gained during my long journey to self-love was a new perspective.

I now know that at the end of my life, I don't want to look back and see all that I missed out on. Life is way too short to be spent wishing you looked different. It is okay to desire to be in better shape, or to be more fit; just don't let that dictate how you live your life. Don't let a few pounds stop you from going after your dream job, starting a new business venture, or going on that date. When I started to live my life, even though my body wasn't perfect, I found happiness.

I still have days that are hard and there are days when I wish I looked different. And that is okay. I catch myself in these moments, and I make the choice to stay in my power. I decide to get back in the driver's seat of my own car and to not give my power away to how I think I should look, or to society's standards.

On the days that I still struggle, I give myself compassion and I speak to my six-year-old self. I tell her that it's okay; she is not a failure and she is beautiful the way she is.

Your journey to loving your body and owning your self-worth will be different from mine. Whatever you do, don't give up hope. The darkest days don't last forever. You will find your body bliss when you let go of how you wish you looked and when you accept and love yourself as you are today. Remember, it is a journey, not a destination. Choose to love yourself EVERY SINGLE DAY, no matter what. Do not give your power away to diet culture, to the impossible standards that are put on us as women, or to your own pursuit of perfection. Your body is incredible. You are beautiful. And you are never ever alone.

In love and health,<br>
Erin Ella<br>
xoxo

# Chapter 7

## FRAN R GARTON

Author Photo: Alicia Thurston Photography
frangartoncoaching.com | IG: @frangartonpaincoach

For as long as I can remember, I've always thought that there was something wrong with my body. Too short, large hips, big breasts, straight hair, big nose, big teeth, large butt. I always found flaws and I was never taught to see the beauty in myself. Indirect comments or "helpful" suggestions were ever present. I spent my life watching all of the women around me worry about their weight, appearance, and how others would judge them. It makes sense that I would grow up with the same viewpoint. I always wished that I looked like my friends. They were beautiful and thin – just perfect. I spent my whole life thinking that I wasn't beautiful. No one ever told me that I wasn't attractive, but no one told me that I was. I came from a loving home and my parents are proud of my accomplishments, but I never felt particularly beautiful. I told myself that I didn't care about dresses, makeup, or being pretty, but looking back, I know that deep down, I cared.

As a way to convince myself that I didn't, I rebelled against traditional norms that would label me as beautiful. As a teenager, I had crazy purple hair, listened to alternative music (think Nine Inch Nails and The Cure) and had unique clothing choices. My style was Goth and I loved it. I was born in Toronto, but went to high school in a very small town and I was considered a weirdo. I remember being called a freak in high school on a regular basis, but I didn't really care. I marched to my own drumbeat, and if people wanted to join me, great. If they didn't, they could kiss my ass! That's the attitude I had through my teen years and into my 30s. Being a freak was a great shield, and it was the perfect way of not having to live up to others' expectations about how I should look or behave. At the time, I thought it was showing my individuality – and it was, to a certain degree – but it was also a way to hide my perceived flaws, to avoid being judged, and to avoid having to face my insecurities.

Throughout my life, I heard many statements that still make me cringe:

"What will everyone think?"

"What will people say about you?"

"Don't you want people to think you're pretty?"

Every time I coloured my hair or bought a unique piece of clothing, I would hear these questions, and I gave the same answer: I don't care. People will say what they want anyway, so I'm not going to try to please them. I told myself that I was smart, so I didn't have to be pretty. I have two Master's Degrees, a teaching certification, had a 16-year teaching career, helped educate people about discriminaton and racism, and now run a successful coaching business. I didn't have many boyfriends and didn't get married until I was 35. I spent most of my teenage years without a boyfriend and I truly believed it was because I wasn't attractive enough, skinny enough... you know, the typical teenage ideas.

Doesn't that statement make you sad? TYPICAL TEENAGE IDEAS. Isn't it tragic that you know exactly what I mean? Why is it acceptable for girls to have this internal dialogue in which they compare themselves to their friends, or magazine and television images? These thoughts are like a computer program running in the background of our lives, and if we're lucky, at some point we uninstall that program, but it takes a lot of work. It's taken over 30 years to see my worthiness and to believe that I'm beautiful – and some days I still have doubts. I'm still working on loving myself, but I've learned a few things that I hope can help you on your journey to love and accept yourself. It wasn't until I was diagnosed with Fibromyalgia that I started to seriously question some of the ridiculous ideas that had burdened me my whole life. My diagnosis was a struggle – and still is – but it is also a blessing in so many ways.

For almost a decade, I suffered through cycles of inflammation and pain. Flare ups were regular occurrences and I wasn't sure how to break the cycle. The best I could do was to plan for my flare ups, recover as best I could, and prepare for the cycle to start again. I didn't change my activities or the intensity of what I did. I just learned how to deal with the ups and downs.

Without knowing what was going on, things were more scattered and uncertain than any other time in my life. I felt absolute terror when I thought about my future. How would I cope? Would my husband still love me? Would I be able to continue working? Would I still be beautiful? Would I have to change careers? I felt panicked thinking about how I would ever be able to achieve my dreams. The inability to breathe was probably the strongest feeling I had living with this uncertainty. It felt like there was an elephant sitting on my chest, and I was being pulled under a huge wave at the same time. I was struggling to reach the surface, but the elephant kept pushing me under.

For the next couple of years, I had increasing difficulty recovering after a workout and had a few minor but recurring injuries. I was exhausted and irritable. Sleep was an intangible entity and utter exhaustion was my everyday reality. Pain was constant and I felt like I was always on the brink of collapsing. The pain range goes from 1 (almost no pain) to 10 (maximum pain). I would pray that my pain level would stay at a 6 because that was what I had learned to live with. I could get through my day at pain level 6. You see, people who suffer from chronic pain hide it. We're ashamed. We're scared. No one will believe us. When I tried to explain the extent of my pain, people would say, "Yes, I know you're in pain. I understand how you feel." But they didn't really know. They couldn't understand its severity. Eventually, I just started saying that I was fine, or I would minimize how I talked about my pain until I finally couldn't – until I didn't have the strength anymore.

My Fibromyalgia actually started presenting itself around 2011, but my diagnosis didn't come until a few years later. A Fibromyalgia diagnosis often takes many years, which leads to immense frustration, fatigue, irritability, and general unpleasantness. In 2011, I was under extreme stress at work, which caused vision loss and intense migraines that put me in bed for four months. It was so severe that doctors thought I might have a brain tumour, cancer, or Multiple Sclerosis. I was terrified. I couldn't even wrap my mind around the possibility of such life-altering diagnoses.

I was relieved to find out that my vision loss would heal itself, but I didn't realize how difficult it would be to rest and recover. I spent much of that time sleeping and crying. I felt utter despair and didn't know how I'd get back to being healthy. My relationship with my husband suffered and we grew apart. I became his patient and he my caregiver. I felt like I wasn't a whole person and that I didn't matter. Even though my husband cared for me and helped me heal, I always felt like I wasn't strong enough; like I wasn't worthy of being well. Even after all these years, there are moments that I still feel like I'm not worthy of being whole. Once I recovered, I thought everything would go back to normal because I was "healed" and had made significant life and work changes. Was I ever wrong! That bout of illness was just the beginning.

The pinnacle of pain was 2013. My pain level of 6 had become 9 and frequently 10. My pain was unbearable, but life goes on and so did I. My feet continually ached, making it difficult to sleep. I rested and napped when I could, but nothing eliminated the constant pain. My pain felt like intense bolts of electricity shooting through my arms, legs, hands, and feet. I'd fall asleep only to be jolted awake from the electricity running wildly through my body. It hurt to walk, to sit, to sleep, to do anything, but I'm a *bit* stubborn, so I just continued with my regular activities. I managed as best I could, because isn't that what we're taught to do? Push through the pain. It can't be that bad. No one understood because no one could feel what I felt. So, I just continued to "live" as best I could.

The summer of 2013 was my breaking point. I just couldn't manage anymore. I was at roller derby practice and I suddenly collapsed in the middle of the track due to weakness. The pain was all-consuming and I couldn't fight through it any longer. My teammates had to swerve around me because I couldn't move myself off the track. I heard the swoosh of their skates and thought they'd come crashing into me at any moment. It felt like my body was made of concrete. I was sobbing because my foot pain was excruciating. I eventually managed to crawl off the track and sat on the ground sobbing from the intensity. I couldn't get my skates off because my hands wouldn't work. I couldn't get off the ground because my body couldn't lift me up. I just sat there and wept.

After my collapse, my family doctor prescribed an anti-inflammatory, a pain killer, and a sleep aid. There were other factors contributing to my pain, which I didn't know at the time. The medication worked for awhile, but I didn't want to be dependent on it, so I decided that I would try to wean myself off my meds. Big mistake. I don't recommend it. The amount of pain was indescribable. I couldn't drive, pick things up, carry groceries, or walk very far because of the pain. Everyday activities were a challenge. I felt like a shell of a person: useless in every way.

Eventually, I had a bone scan and saw a Rheumatologist who diagnosed my Fibromyalgia. Apparently, I was a textbook case (not sure I agree). If so, why did it take so long to figure out what was going on?! I was completely annoyed and frustrated. Getting my Fibromyalgia diagnosis felt like a blessing, but also a curse because it consumed all my thoughts. I did what most people would do: research. I read everything that I could find, searched all the websites, and read as many books as I could. I had friends with Fibromyalgia, so I reached out to them. I wanted insights, suggestions, and help. The Mayo Clinic defines Fibromyalgia as a disorder characterized by widespread musculoskeletal pain accompanied by fatigue, sleep, memory, and mood issues. Researchers believe that Fibromyalgia amplifies painful sensations by affecting the way our brain and spinal cord process painful and non-painful signals. No real cause has ever been found. There is no real treatment. No cure. I need to learn to live with it. Really?! Unhelpful and frustrating.

Everyone I spoke with gave the same advice:

It sucks.

It's painful.

Give up doing the things you love.

Take your meds. If they don't work, try different ones.

Prepare for flare ups.

Hope for the best.

*WORST ADVICE EVER!*

There must be another way. People just don't give everything up and suffer... well, maybe THEY do, but I certainly wasn't going to. I'm a Virgo for crying out loud! Virgos don't give up; we just find another way!

Despite my condition, I did whatever activity I wanted and dealt with the aches and pains that followed. Sometimes it was agonizing pain and extreme discomfort from anything touching my skin. Other times it was the difficulty with walking and using my hands. Standing up or holding a glass or attempting to eat were challenging, to say the least. The worst was having to stay in bed because I didn't have the strength to endure the pain of getting up. I had to miss work and social events, but in my mind I wanted to push through. I couldn't miss out on life because of my diagnosis, so I persisted and often did things despite the intense pain.

I believed that's how things were supposed to be: pain with a few recovery days. My recovery began taking longer and the pain and inflammation increased in intensity. I assumed that the cycle I was in was the natural progression as I got closer to 40. To be honest, I didn't really think that getting older was going to hold me back from doing things that I wanted to do. I started roller derby when I was in my late 30s, so I didn't believe age mattered or altered what I could achieve or do. I believed that my body might be more sore or take longer to heal, but aside from that, I didn't let age or my diagnosis define what I could do.

My perspective on my body and movement has definitely changed, and it's been a long journey to get here. Now, I'm ecstatic to say that I'm thriving despite my Fibromyalgia and generally my pain level is at a 1 most days, but it wasn't always this way. I've learned a few lessons that helped me shift the way I view my body and to accept myself as I am.

## LESSON #1: DON'T LIVE IN THE PAST

In the past, I could choose any exercise style, engage at maximum intensity, and recover quite easily. I would have typical aches and pains that came with exercising, but I didn't spend much time thinking about how my body would respond to movement before I actually moved.

Having Fibromyalgia meant that my body didn't recover like it used to and the pain would be intense with even the smallest amount of movement. Muscle soreness lasted for days and kept me in bed. Headaches increased in frequency and nothing would help them subside. I would wake up dreading how my body would feel. It was terrifying and exhausting. It took a long time to accept the idea that I had to plan my movement. I had to anticipate how I might feel, and in turn, how that would impact my day. Plans were cancelled, appointments rescheduled, time with friends and family didn't happen, and sick days had to be used – all because I tried new activities. The problem wasn't movement; it was my perspective. I was anticipating the ways that my body would fail me rather than embracing the ways that my body was allowing me to move. I was focusing on the things I used to be able to do rather than opening my mind to the new things that I could try.

Now I wake up feeling like I am reborn every day. I get to listen to my body and then decide what my movement for the day will be. I say yes to so many new activities that I wouldn't have ever thought about trying in the past. I get to say no to any movement that doesn't make me feel good and I don't feel shame or guilt about saying no. I am also blessed with the time to see how my body responds and to decide to continue or move on to something else. I've learned that my body loves to move, but it needs time – to respond, adjust, enjoy, and recover. I've been able to try Animal Flow, Mace Training, various yoga styles, QiGong, Tai Chi, line dancing, chair workouts, and I even trained for a half marathon. I've been given time to choose the movement that I love. This has been a great learning experience and one that I teach to others. Movement should be enjoyable and make you feel good. Living in the past only focuses on what WAS, instead of focusing on what can BE in the future.

## LESSON #2: HEAL YOURSELF

Getting diagnosed with Fibromyalgia sent me on a journey of education and knowledge focusing on medication, food, movement, sleep, and stress reduction. There were many negative emotions: fear, anger, resentment, sadness, and grief. Dealing with these emotions is overwhelming and it's much easier to control the symptoms with medication instead of dealing with the causes. Fibromyalgia is not a progressive disease, which means that it won't get worse over time. However, dealing with and eliminating or minimizing triggers is the key to effective pain management. It took a lot of hard work, failures, and sacrifices to make it as far as I have in thriving despite my Fibromyalgia.

Reducing and eliminating things that caused flare ups was extremely helpful and worked for quite a while, but it wasn't a complete solution. Approaching a problem from a medical perspective gives you medical solutions; a nutrition perspective gives nutrition solutions, and so on. Each methodology has its merits, but flare ups and intense pain continued and I seemed to have exhausted my pain management options. However, I still felt like there had to be another solution. I widened my search and started to look at the connection between emotions and pain. We experience emotions in our bodies, and if we hold onto negative emotions, they manifest as pain in our body. Think about when you have an intense headache. The more you focus on it, the worse it gets. But if you're able to distract yourself and focus on something else, the headache is minimized or disappears completely.

As I researched the pain-emotion connection, I found the same information: work on the inside, heal your emotions, and forgive others and yourself. Could it really be that simple? Now, if you've gone through this process, you know it is absolutely anything but simple. It's actually hard AF! But after many tears, lots of work on myself, and tons of forgiveness, I've come out on the other side and my pain is almost completely gone, and anything above a 3 has me questioning and investigating what's actually causing my pain. Emotions are connected to pain. **Forgiving and releasing past emotions, trauma, anger, fear, and resentment is the only way to release pain.** To GET through it, you have to GO through it. When you're doing the work on yourself, it sucks and it's hard, but once it's done, you won't believe how amazing you feel. But you need to do the work. No one can do it for you. You can read all the books, attend the workshops, watch and listen to the advice, but until you actually dig deep and DO the work, you won't get the results you seek. You'll get close, but the positive results will be temporary. **Instead of pretending to heal yourself, actually take the time and space you need to go through the work, and with every layer you uncover and release, another one comes to the surface.** Feel the emotions, understand why they are there, and then release them. There are so many positive emotions and experiences in life, so why hold onto the negative, painful ones?

## LESSON #3: MY BODY IS AMAZING

For most of my life, I took for granted all of the things that my body could do. Well, actually, I just assumed that my body would always work as I commanded it to without consequence. If my body couldn't do something, I would either try harder or move on to something else. Even though I struggled to love myself for many years, I was confident in my body's abilities and the certainty that I could condition my body to do what I asked of it. My body was healthy, resilient, and strong. Then, after my diagnosis, I started to focus on the things that I couldn't do. I would pine for activities I had once enjoyed, or the carefree way that I used to say yes to any new adventure. I would spend time agonizing and envisioning all of the ways that my body would rebel – how my pain would flare up, or prepare to be in bed for days.

But today, I realize that my body is amazing. It's been through so much and it's still going strong. I've survived injuries, fractures, concussions, setbacks, vision loss, recurring migraines, extreme nausea, muscle tears, Fibromyalgia, Osteoarthritis, and days in bed recovering from flare ups, but my body still heals itself and I usually feel strong and healthy. **My body doesn't give up on me, so I can't give up on it, either.** I wake up every morning and feel grateful to be alive, blessed to be able to serve my clients, and I live with joy and love. My body didn't let me down. I let my body down. I ignored the messages to slow down and make changes. I kept pushing myself until my body finally got tired of being ignored and I was forced to stop. Now, I listen and recognize the signals before it's too late. And when I listen carefully, my body tells me that it loves me and that I'm enough.

## LESSON #4: TRUE LOVE EXISTS

It took me a really long time to find true love, and it was seriously tested by my vision loss and my diagnosis. I'm not talking about the romantic kind of love that you see in the movies. I'm talking about the kind of love that sticks around during the really crappy times. True love isn't only about sex, romance, and happiness. It's really about the arguments, uncertainty, fear, tears, sadness, and loss. True love is about the hard times and the in-between times when you're just not sure what's going to happen next. And you don't know you've got true love until it's actually tested by the monumentally challenging times.

My husband is a saint and I truly mean that. He has dealt with me and my Fibromyalgia over the years while I tried to navigate my wellness, and he does it with calmness and compassion. However, as hard as he tries, he can never understand exactly what I mean when I say I'm exhausted or am in pain. He says he does, and here's the impact: I'm like a fire-breathing dragon from the depths of hell when he says, "I know you're in pain." or "I know you're exhausted." No, he doesn't. He can't possibly understand how much pain I have or how exhausted I truly feel. I know he's trying, but it just pisses me off. It truly does. People with Fibromyalgia never get a break from utter exhaustion. Having a nap, getting dressed, or taking a shower makes me tired. It never ends. So, when my husband says he knows how I feel, my dragon raises her head and gets ready to torch things! Exhaustion makes me grumpy, irritable, short-tempered, frustrated, and angry… and to be honest, these emotions rise so quickly I don't realize what I'm doing or saying. My Fibromyalgia causes arguments between my husband and I that, at times, I fear it will destroy us. I try really hard to keep my dragon happy and calm, and other times I'm so fucking tired that I just can't be bothered.

My dragon led me to constantly worry that my husband would leave me, and this fed into the idea that I'm not worthy of love. I didn't think that he could love someone who had Fibromyalgia. I thought that as I aged, my body would change, and so potentially would the things I could do, which in turn would lead him to leave me.

My view of my body and my beauty has been seriously tested by my Fibromyalgia. How could I be beautiful to someone when I'm irritable?! How could I be attractive when my body aches so much that I don't want to be touched?! How can I sustain a marriage when I can't muster up enough energy to get out of bed, let alone have enough energy for sex?! But through it all, my husband has stood by me. At times, I know he's wondered why he's still here. I can only assume that he must truly love me. He must see and remember my great qualities underneath all of my scales that shine so brightly during a flare up! See… there's that little voice creeping in, making me doubt my beauty and worthiness. **It's a constant battle to rewrite the "not good enough" narrative**. I oscillate between loving who I am today, and not feeling worthy enough to be accepted. Having my husband by my side showing me what true love looks like helps me through my toughest days.

Fibromyalgia has taught me so many lessons and delivered many blessings. Over the past decade, I have been redefining not only who I am, but also who I choose to be. I got to Level 50 this year and I realized that I've got so much more living to do – and I want to do it with happiness, joy, and ease. The best way that I know how to do that is to stop trying to fit into someone else's limited definition of who I should be and how I should look. I have the power to create the life I want. I just need to have the courage to reach for it. I'm perfect just the way I am, and so are you. Don't you dare listen to anyone who tells you anything different. Be who you are meant to be. Love who you are today!

INSTEAD OF PRETENDING TO HEAL YOURSELF, ACTUALLY TAKE THE TIME AND SPACE YOU NEED TO GO THROUGH THE WORK, AND WITH EVERY LAYER YOU UNCOVER AND RELEASE, ANOTHER ONE COMES TO THE *surface.*

# *Chapter 8*

# JENNIFER HEARD

AUTHOR PHOTO: ALICIA THURSTON PHOTOGRAPHY
IG: @drojen7

Not too long ago, anytime I looked in a mirror, I would think to myself, "How the fuck did I get here? I used to be pretty. I used to look so much better." I have one small mirror in my house for this very reason – I hated seeing my reflection. I'm carrying 70-100 pounds more weight than I have in the past. I've got a wonky front tooth (a prime example of how I was not taking care of myself). I got an infection behind the tooth that eventually pushed it out and down. I'm lucky I didn't lose it… yet. I hate that tooth and what it symbolizes to me. I have spent hours berating myself for "letting myself go." And you know what I've finally realized? I didn't let myself go. I was trying to survive and was desperately hanging on!

I went through a major depressive episode not too long ago that brought me to a place that I never want to be again, having thoughts I never want to have again. Eventually, I reached a turning point. When you've been in a place where you just wish you could disappear, that you would do almost anything to make the pain and hurt of feeling blamed, shamed, and judged by some of the people closest to you go away, I don't think you can make your way out of it and not be forever changed.

I made it through and some things will never be the same. I hope not. Now I know that I am enough, just as I am, right here, right now. I deserve to be happy and healthy. I work every day to accept myself, my body, and my mind as it is right now. I don't need to prove my worth to anyone anymore. Accept me, warts and all, or there is no place for you in my life.

Does that mean that I'm not going to try to lose some of those 70-100 pounds? Nope, because I know I can accept my body right now AND want to lose weight to be the healthiest version of myself that I can be. What I have learned is that if I don't accept myself where I am right now, I won't suddenly accept myself because I'm 20, 30, 40, or more pounds lighter. I have to accept what I see and how I feel right now.

My name is Jennifer Heard. I'm an Accounting Officer, a single mom to an amazing young man who happens to have special needs, a powerlifter and gym enthusiast, and now, I am an author!

My journey is just beginning. You may be wondering how I got here. It's been a long, bumpy road. I grew up in a small town in Ontario, the middle of three children. I was never the smallest girl in the room. I remember being called fat at school. I was shy, awkward, and insecure. Kids are great at sensing who would be a great target, and I definitely was a target on occasion. I never really felt that I fit in anywhere, nor did I feel that I was particularly good at anything.

We were raised as many were in those days – to clean our plates. If we took it, we ate it. Fresh vegetables were plentiful in the summer because we had our own garden. In the winter, it was canned, sometimes frozen. Regardless, veggies were basic: peas, beans, carrots, potatoes, corn, leaf lettuce, and spinach (summer only). And I'm sorry, Mom, they were always cooked until just shy of mush (if we were lucky). It was just the way things were cooked then. Meat was cooked until DONE. I grew up thinking that I only liked ground beef and chicken (fried – thank you, Dixie Lee). Honestly, I didn't know that turkey could taste good until a few years ago! I still can't bring myself to eat roast beef, steak, or pork chops.

I also remember that every January, my mom and dad would go on a diet. When I look back on it now, I can see it was always my dad's idea; my mom went along with it, but was never 100% committed. My dad would go all out and drop weight quickly and my mom would struggle. I remember two staples of their diet were ½ a grapefruit for breakfast and melba toast. I learned early that diets were something you did once a year, that they were a struggle, and they included food you hated. I mean, truly, melba toast is the equivalent of tree bark to me! Hello early '70s diet culture! This is where my ideas about food and diet began.

I look back at pictures of myself in high school and I see a girl who really wasn't much bigger than anyone else, yet I remember feeling so fat, so ugly, so not enough. It doesn't help that I was called fat often.

After high school, I moved to the big city of Toronto. I lived there for 12 years and life was pretty fun for many of those years. I had an okay job, I had some great friends, and I was living in the big city! I ended up in a relationship that was, at times, quite volatile and very messed up. I was in that relationship, off and on, for several years. The end result was a surprise pregnancy and a permanent, much needed end to that relationship. He opted out. He wanted no part of being a dad. I allowed him to go. I knew it was best for my baby. I figured I would be okay with the support of my parents. I didn't anticipate their reaction. To say they were not happy might be an understatement. I was told that no one would help me, and that we would probably starve to death. My stubborn streak was triggered. I decided I would show everyone that I did not need anyone and I would never ask for help.

The pregnancy was normal with no issues. The birth was relatively quick, completely natural, and uneventful. We were released from the hospital to go home to an empty apartment – just the two of us. I had no idea what I was doing, but I'd been told that no one would help us, so I wasn't about to ask for any. I had difficulty getting him to nurse, and finally my midwives came for a home visit. At four days old, they had us return to the hospital to have some things checked out. He seemed to have lost too much weight and they were a little concerned. We were admitted to the hospital and tests began. Finally, on day five, they realized that he was having seizures, over and over again. They weren't sure if he was going to survive. He was rushed to Sick Kids. I had to call my family to tell them if they wanted to see him, they better come, because he might not make it. My family came immediately. At nine days old, I was told that he had brain damage, and would likely be completely blind and never walk. I remember holding that little boy in my arms and thinking to myself, *You are wrong, he will walk. He will do anything he sets his mind to. I know he will.*

I decided we should move to Kitchener, where my sister lived. It was the best decision I ever made. Here, eventually, I could afford to buy a house on my own, he received needed services much faster, and getting around was a lot easier than it would have been in Toronto. I settled in and concentrated on getting my son to be everything he could be. Turns out, he is stubborn like me. He is not completely blind and he not only walks, he runs, skates, rides a bike, lifts heavy weight, and has no idea he could possibly have a limitation. He walked late, at almost two-and-a-half. He has some cognitive delays and he does have a visual impairment, but in a familiar environment, you would never know it.

We settled into our life – just him and I. I devoted myself to him. I didn't feel like I had the time, energy, or ability to strike up friendships with people. I didn't feel that I had much to offer, and my son came first.

I was always an emotional eater. Happy, sad, angry – if it was an emotion, I ate it. Food became my friend, my companion, my comfort. It was always there for me and it never let me down. So I ate. And I ate. And I ate. The more I ate, the more I started feeling negatively about myself – not good enough, not smart enough, not trying hard enough. So I ate some more, and I lost myself. I was never good in social situations, but I completely lost any ability to strike up a conversation with someone. I isolated myself. The friends I had in Toronto were around at first, but life marches on and things change. That's just what happens with distance and time. I went back to work when he was seven months old, and that was my life for the next several years: work and doing everything that I could to get him to meet those milestones. I had no time for outside friends or interests of my own.

It was several years before I made friends here. I had my sister and her family, but I often felt like we were invading their space and time if we went over too frequently. When Jordan was three, I bought our little townhouse and ended up five minutes away from my work and his daycare. When he was six, he started school at the School for the Blind in Brantford and was bussed back and forth every day.

Once he was old enough, I started getting him involved in the Special Olympics and then a local hockey team for people with special needs. As he got older, I got a little more comfortable leaving him alone at home for short periods of time. I took up running thanks to my cousin Jo-Anne and a program called Couch to 5K. I ran in the early morning hours around the sidewalk of our townhouse complex parking lot. I ran then because my son would be asleep, but mostly because no one would see me. I didn't want anyone to actually see me running! All those bits and pieces bouncing around? Oh Hell no! I trained for a 5K and ran it with my cousin. She'd told me runners were all shapes and sizes, but I didn't believe it until that day. They really are! I didn't feel judged for my appearance or size at all.

I trained for a 10k the next year and then piriformis syndrome sidelined my running for a while. The last race I did was a ½ marathon. That was quite an accomplishment, and yet I experienced some letdown afterwards. Even though I hadn't gone in without any real expectations other than to finish it, I felt like I hadn't done well enough. I felt disappointed in myself even though I finished in just under three hours.

One thing that I learned during this period is that physical activity has a direct relationship to my mental health. I need it or I start to feel sad. I found ways to stay somewhat active from this point on.

My son did several sports with the Special Olympics over the years, but the one that changed both of our lives the most was powerlifting. This program ran at one gym for a couple of years, but it was when it moved to a different gym that changed everything for me. They started really doing powerlifting at this gym. Who knew watching these athletes learn to do the "Big Three" – bench, back squat, and deadlift – would send me down the next leg of my path to body acceptance? This gym also ran programming two nights a week for people with special needs, which I also got my son involved in. They were so welcoming and so accepting of him that they encouraged me to do the adult classes after his classes and he could just hang out and wait for me to be done.

Then one day, after helping out at a powerlifting meet for our special needs group, I started thinking that maybe I wanted to learn how to powerlift too. I kept the idea to myself for a while, but eventually I asked the owner what I should do to get started. She gave me some pointers and I started powerlifting on Friday nights while my son was doing his class. For me, there was nothing like getting under a barbell and lifting it. It is empowering in a way that I never would have guessed it would be. I loved it. I kept working on the three lifts, setting some goals for myself along the way for the next four months. Then, I started thinking about competing, again, keeping the thought to myself for a while. Then, someone suggested that I train for a competition.

With a lot of support and encouragement from the gym, I started to train alongside a good friend who agreed to train with me. They even provided me with my programming. I trained hard for several months. The people at the gym knew what I was doing, but my immediate family didn't. Some still don't know. Why? Well, all of those thoughts about not being enough going around in my head come from somewhere, don't they? I felt I would be teased, laughed at, judged, discouraged – any number of things that would not have helped me stay focused, and honestly probably would have meant me giving up. Scratch that. It would have *definitely* meant giving up. Plus, if something happened and I was unable to do it, I wouldn't have to worry about anyone saying "we knew you couldn't do it." So I kept it to myself.

I participated in my first powerlifting meet in 2019. It was a women's-only event and it was a great experience. Let me tell you, standing out there on a platform in front of a whole bunch of strangers in a singlet that hides absolutely nothing took a great deal of courage for me. It was inspiring to be surrounded by like-minded, strong women of all shapes and sizes who could lift some serious weight!

I did well, hitting or surpassing previous one rep maxes. I went in thinking that I had no expectations but to just lift what I could and do my best. However, for some reason, I felt let down afterwards. Those thoughts came up again: *You didn't lift enough. You should have done more. You let yourself and everyone else down.* I confessed my feelings to my friend and training partner, and she told me that I was not being fair to myself. I knew she was right.

I had made a deal with myself to just have fun and enjoy the experience with no expectations. I thought I had, but my feelings afterward told me a different story. It was just like the feelings I had after my ½ marathon. I didn't feel like I deserved to be proud of myself. I fell into a bit of a funk for a while after that and never really told anyone else about my post-meet feelings. I pulled myself out of it and carried on.

I even started to train for another competition that was to take place in June 2020. Then COVID came along, and then injuries started: my left hip, my right shoulder, my right knee, my left hamstring, and finally my right elbow. Competitions were cancelled due to COVID by this time, so I took some time away from that intense training.

I fell into another funk. This one started out like any other, except I couldn't seem to pull myself out. Going to the gym – my sanctuary – became very difficult to do. I kept going because it was the one outlet for my son. His only human interaction occurred at the gym, thanks to COVID, and I couldn't take that away from him. It caused me a lot of anxiety to be there, though, and I just wanted to get in and out again and not talk to anyone. I didn't want to have to pretend to be okay, and I didn't want to be asked what was wrong. I was on the verge of tears every time I walked in the door and I couldn't explain why. I had no answer. Still don't, to be honest. I was just sad. I shut people out and I shut myself down as much as I could. I left the gym every single night and cried in my car on the way home. Some people gave me space, thinking I was just sad about the injuries, some people reached out, and others turned their backs on me. I became too much for some of the people closest to me. The funk went deeper than it ever had before and I was alone, trying to figure it out, while still keeping my shit together for my son.

After Christmas, another lockdown came into effect. At least I didn't have to pretend at the gym anymore. Online classes were offered, which I had my son do, but I'd bought some programming and was doing that on my own, at my own pace, and at a time of day that suited me. My physical injuries started to heal and I started trying to figure out what to do about the relationships that had changed because I'd gotten depressed and was dealing with it in the way that many people who get depressed deal with it. I started reading books, trying to learn more about myself and figure out how to help myself. I went to therapy for a while, too.

I wanted to figure out why I had those thoughts on a loop in my head. Why did I feel like I had to apologize to people for feeling a sadness I couldn't explain? Why was I willing to put up with people who left me feeling blamed, shamed, and judged – for having those feelings? Why didn't I feel like I was enough, just as I am? Why didn't I feel like I deserved some understanding?

The turning point came when, once again, I found myself apologizing to a (now former) friend for my sadness, for my anxiety, and for hurting her feelings, while never once getting acknowledgement for the pain that I felt she had caused me. After that, I hit rock bottom. It was a long and lonely time for me, and my feelings during that time scared me.

Then I got a text from another (now former) friend, saying that she'd heard things were going well between that other friend and me. I'd been feeling the lowest I'd ever felt in my life; I didn't really consider that "going well." Then I got angry. I *did* deserve better! Not just from others, but from *myself*. I was going to start giving myself better. I was going to give myself whatever I needed. If that meant losing people who I felt had shamed, blamed, and judged me, so be it.

I started journaling. I started with three pages. The first was positive affirmations. The second was things that I was grateful for, and the third was things that I liked about myself. I made an agreement with myself that for 30 days, I was going to write one thing on each of those pages every day. I felt stupid at first. It was unnatural to give myself compliments and grace, but as the days progressed, I started to feel better and better. More positive, happier. Remembering what you have to be grateful for and the things that are good about yourself is empowering. I was a different person after 30 days. I realized that the final conversation with that former friend was a blessing. I realized that it freed me so that I could remember who I am. It was time for me to work on myself. I don't think I would be doing this chapter in this book if those friendships had not fallen apart.

I knew that I needed to accept myself for who I am, what I look like right now, and that losing 80 pounds was not going to change my perception of myself. I was 100 pounds lighter 25 years ago, and it did not make my life better. I still had those "not good enough" thoughts on a loop. I was in that volatile relationship, and I still felt insecure – possibly even more so at 100 pounds lighter. I've learned that I have to accept myself right now, as I am.

I'm not going to lie and say that I'll never try to lose weight again. I am trying to lose weight; I know that I need to for my health. Heart attacks, strokes, and diabetes are very much a part of my family history. I have to make better choices for that reason.

The difference this time is that it is not about that number on the scale. I can still get invested in that number – but, now when I do, I stop weighing myself for a while and refocus on making sure my food is nutritious fuel for my body. I don't punish myself with food when I feel sad or lonely or hurt in some way. If I want a piece of cake, I eat that piece of cake and I don't feel guilty about it or feel like I have to starve myself the next day. I've started to think of food as fuel, not as a reward or punishment – nor do I use it to eat my feelings. I feel my feelings (hello journal!) and fuel with food.

I've learned that too much sugar sends my mood plummeting as well. It is not good for my mental health. If I don't eat well, I don't feel well. I am learning to love my strong body that can squat 225 lbs, bench press 135 lbs, and deadlift 265 lbs – just as it is. I want to love it now so that I can love it always, no matter what size it wears. Size is just another number, after all. It doesn't matter any more than your shoe size matters.

I continue to go to the gym. My original gym has now closed, which is for the best. While I will be forever grateful for everything that was done for both myself and my son, for all I learned there, and for those two former friends who were a part of that gym – it is a relief to have no further connection. I've moved on to another gym.

My feelings on exercise have changed. Now, it is about movement. I just want to move in a way that feels good to me. I am still lifting weight, I'm just not as focussed on going heavy like I used to. I am open to moving in whatever way my body and mind want to move on any given day. I listen to what my body is telling me when it comes to food, nutrition, and movement. It's not exercise any more. It's simply movement, whatever that looks like on any given day. Will I compete again? I'm really not sure. As of this moment, I don't feel the need to push my body that hard again. I am reserving the right to change my mind on this, though.

At the end of the day, I know that I am enough, right here, right now. I am a strong, independent woman who has raised an amazing young man, who happens to have special needs, to be a kind, giving, caring individual who always has a smile and a hug for the people who mean something to him. I own my own home. I have worked 20 years for the same company and I am good at my job. I look at myself in the mirror now. I used to avoid it. I look at myself objectively and when a negative thought comes into my mind, I choose to replace it with a positive one. Instead of *OMG, look at the size of that butt*, I think, *OMG, look at the strength you carry in that butt. That butt can help you lift just about anything that you need to lift.*

I know that I still have work to do. As I lose weight, my body is going to change. I'm 53, so things are not going to snap back into place. There will be things that are going to make me sad: loose skin, saggy bits, flappy arms. I will continue to work on accepting all of those things, because my body – everyone's body – is amazing. Our bodies are a part of our story. Our bodies can carry human beings. Our bodies can comfort us when we need comfort. Our bodies are strong for us when we need them to be strong. Our bodies can move in so many amazing ways. Our bodies deserve to be accepted for what they do for us every single day. The journey to body acceptance is hard, but so is staying where you are. My journey has just begun, and I am excited to see where it takes me.

MY BODY DOESN'T
GIVE UP ON ME, SO I CAN'T
GIVE UP ON IT, *either.*

# Chapter 9

# JILLIAN GRANT

AUTHOR PHOTO: ALICIA THURSTON PHOTOGRAPHY
IG: @wwjillmaura

Fear of the number on the scale or the size of the pants that I wear has programmed my mind and actions for many years. Were my fears valid? Yes. Were they healthy? No, not for me. Hello friends, my name is Jillian. This is my story about how I started – and continue – my wellness journey to becoming a healthier, happier version of myself.

I have always been insecure, and I was seen as "overweight" by society. I was always on the heavier side and accepted it early on in my teenage life. Or, at least I thought that I had accepted it.

I always found the largest sizes in the stores. I hid behind people in photos. I always wore long shorts or pants, and rarely would I wear something that showed my shoulders. Events with family and friends were a regular part of my life, but I always hid the fact that I was afraid of embarrassment and what others would think of me if I participated in certain activities. This was how I lived my life.

My entire life changed when I had a near death experience. What was meant to be an exciting adventure ended up being an "a-ha moment" that changed my mindset about my state of wellness. I was visiting friends in Calgary, and we decided to go white water rafting in Banff. Sounds fun, right? Well, when it was my turn to be fitted for a wetsuit, the person assisting said, "Oh, you will need an XXL. Let me see if we have one that's big enough for you." Then, he or she yelled to another employee, "Hey, do we have any larger wetsuits? This lady needs one."

And instantly – embarrassment! I turned around to see a dozen or more people in line staring at me. It took everything in me not to scream or bawl my eyes out. Instead, I took the suit, went into the change area, and cried in private. I asked myself, *Wow. Should I even be going on this rafting trip? What did I get myself into? They don't even have a suit that's my size!* I felt horrible, but I tried to brush it off and enjoy the time with my friends.

But, of course, a second incident would occur that was equally as embarrassing. While rafting, I fell out of the boat into the river and struggled to get above the water. I remember thinking at that moment, "This is the end. How do I get above the water?" I could barely breathe. I was struggling to swim, but I got above the water. Then, I heard people laughing. They thought I was having fun. In reality, I was just happy to be alive. I laughed along with them so they couldn't see my embarrassment, and so I wouldn't feel like the laughingstock of the adventure, even though I was.

As if that wasn't bad enough, now I needed to get back into the boat. It took four people to lift me back into the boat as I struggled to pull myself up and not make an even bigger scene than it already was.

In the end, I was scared and embarrassed. It took away from the experience that I was trying to have with my friends. I felt uncomfortable in my own skin. I was embarrassed to go anywhere or do anything during the trip because the rafting incident affected my confidence and self-esteem. I really wanted to just hide away and not do anything fun. This whole experience made me realize that I needed to make a change. I decided then that I would invest more energy and time into my wellness and focus on myself and my wellbeing. I was going to shift my lifestyle choices completely.

When I returned home, I started researching different weight loss options, and I spoke with people who recently went through a weight loss journey of their own. I decided to start using a weight loss/wellness app to track my weight, eating habits, and activities. My first thought was, *I need to lose*

*100 pounds. That is my goal.* I was scared, suffering from self-doubt, embarrassed, and overall nervous for these major changes that I was about to make in my life. I wasn't sure if I could do it. How long could I keep it up? Can I even do it? I knew that the first step was weighing myself. Ugh, I was dreading this moment. I stepped on the scale and started to cry. I felt like the number was yelling at me. 257 pounds! How did I let myself get to 257 pounds? I was embarrassed and overwhelmed. That number felt so scary, but I was taking the first step toward becoming a healthier self.

During the first year of my journey, I focused on tracking my meals and incorporating new, healthier choices. Each week, I would write down small, achievable goals, and I was doing great! I started to figure out what worked for me. I loved trying new recipes, discovering new things, and each week I continued to lose weight. The first week I lost 5.7 pounds. The second week I was down 0.4 pounds. The third week I was down 2.8. And the fourth week, I had shed a total of 11.2 pounds. I was on a roll, and I was determined to keep going. The numbers proved that I was succeeding. In three months, I was down 25 pounds. After 9 months, I had lost 50 pounds, and I was becoming a little irritated that people weren't noticing my weight loss. Where were the comments like, "Wow! Have you lost weight?" As a result, I felt like I wasn't doing enough. How much longer would it take to reach my 100-pound goal? I couldn't wait to be a smaller size.

My partner, now fiancé, Josh, is always so supportive of my journey. I was self-conscious changing in front of him, and I did not want him to see me naked with the lights on. He calls me beautiful regardless of my size, but I didn't feel beautiful then, even after losing the initial weight. I have been a bridesmaid quite a few times in the last ten years (seven times, to be exact). Dress shopping was always uncomfortable, especially with other girls who were smaller than me.

Here is a funny story for you about one of the times that I was a bridesmaid in a friend's wedding: I was going for my last dress fitting, since it was a week before the wedding. Josh came with me to the bridal shop, and we had just started dating at the time. I was waiting for the seamstress and the dress was not fitting. It was tight, and I could barely breathe. I was mad at myself for gaining weight over the last few months. As I held the dress against me, I said to Josh in an angry voice, "It will probably be some skinny little bitch who is going to help me." I was not trying to be offensive at the time, but I was just angry with myself, and I lashed out. Josh had never heard me say something like that and, in fact, I don't even remember saying it. But, Josh reminded me of this story months later when I was well into my wellness journey. Now, he calls me his "skinny little bitch," and we laugh about how that came to be.

I decided to create an Instagram account. Everyone was doing that, right? I thought this would be a new way for me to be more accountable and to connect with people in similar situations as me. I would post the meals that I was eating, new recipe ideas, activities I was getting into, and what I was going through mentally. Basically, I was sharing my overall weight loss experience. Before I knew it, I had become a part of a community, and I gained friends who inspired and motivated me.

I didn't predict the impact that I would have on other people. I was inspiring others by being open and willing to share all aspects of my journey: the good, the bad, and the ugly. I would get messages like, "Thanks for sharing. That really helped me," or "You just made my day by sharing that," or even, "I feel the same way." I found it inspiring and rewarding to watch others transform and hear stories that were like mine. The more I shared, the more confident I felt. I found my people! They were welcoming, encouraging, and interested in my success and well-being. My new Instagram community became the place where I felt comfortable sharing my weight. I had never shared the number on the scale with anyone except my doctor! And even then, I always looked away from the number.

I continued to set and share weekly goals for myself, tracking my meals, and creating meal plans. I also started to move my body more. Each day, I would focus on one or two small goals, like increasing my water intake or getting out for a 15-minute walk. I had reached the halfway point of my weight-loss goal. I was really starting to feel a change, and not just with my physical appearance. My mindset and mental health were changing, too. I was beginning to feel confident. I had found what was helping me reach my goals, and people were noticing my success. They would ask me how I was doing it, which finally started to make me feel like I was succeeding.

A pivotal moment that changed my outlook in this journey was when I finally decided to go and buy new clothes. After losing 50 pounds, my clothes were falling off of me and were too baggy because I had been avoiding shopping for new clothes.

I have always loved, yet hated, shopping – if that is possible. I always look for the best deals, but picking a shirt or pants off of the rack was my least favorite thing to do. I always had to go for the largest size or check to see if

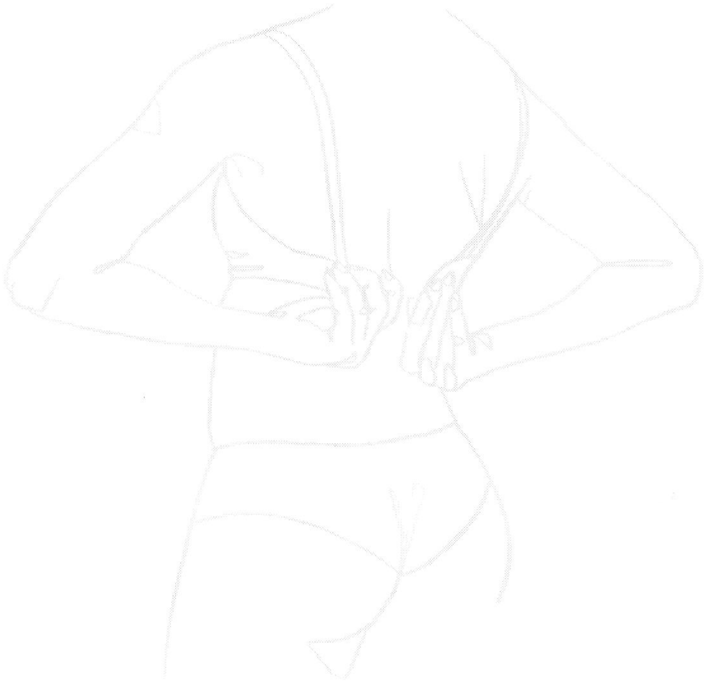

THE *number* ON THE SCALE DOES NOT REPRESENT YOUR WORTH, NOR DOES IT FULLY REFLECT YOUR PROGRESS THROUGH YOUR WELLNESS JOURNEY.

the store even carried my size. I would always walk into the store and if the "plus size" was a separate area in a store, I would feel uncomfortable. Trying on clothes always made me feel less pretty, and less worthy, so I always had clothes that I didn't wear because I would buy clothes without trying them on, just because they were "in my size."

It was summertime, and I picked out a few one-piece swimsuits. I picked out one that was quite revealing, compared to what I would've picked in the past. It actually showed some skin! I went into the dressing room, put it on, looked in the mirror, and cried. In that moment, I felt proud of myself. Damn, I looked good! It was one of the first times that I felt good and sexy in a swimsuit. I needed to buy it! And as a bonus, it was on sale. It felt meant to be.

On that day, the number on the scale didn't matter. I was proud and loved the way I looked in that mirror. I wanted to be able to go to the beach and have the same feelings that I had in the dressing room. Could I really feel confident wearing this bathing suit in public?

Well, I went to the beach wearing that swimsuit, and you know what, my friends? That was the moment. At this point, the scales tipped for me (pun intended!), and I realized that my success was about more than just weight loss; I was creating a wellness lifestyle for myself.

This was the self-love and confidence that I needed to feel. This journey was much more than losing 50 pounds; it was about loving my body the way it was in that moment on the beach. Yes, I did the work to lose the weight, but I realized that I was doing so much more than that. I was finding my confidence and self-worth. Why did I spend so many years being insecure about showing my skin and my body? Now I was loving myself the way that I should have loved myself the whole time, and I was really starting to appreciate my body.

I wanted to advocate for normalizing normal bodies. Stretch marks, skin tags, rolls – these are all very normal parts of many bodies. I started to flaunt my body and become more myself. I wore what I wanted to, and I didn't let anyone tell me otherwise. Society's "norms" had little impact on what clothes I was wearing. I was beginning to love all aspects of my body. I also overcame my fear of changing or being naked in front of my partner. Josh always tries to make me feel comfortable and beautiful with him, and I finally started to trust those feelings with him. I was now confident and poised.

At about twenty-two months into my journey, after lots of work and dedication, I finally stepped on that scale to see that I had reached my goal (or at least what I thought was my goal). I had lost 100 pounds! I did it! I felt so accomplished. That was it; I got to where I wanted to be.

After a few weeks went by, I started slowly gaining pounds back. I still continued with my healthy lifestyle and was doing the things that I had been doing for months, but I was no longer at the 100-pound mark. The truth is, I haven't been back to that number since. You know what, my friends? That is okay! In fact, I learned that the number isn't what is important or what determines my success, it is how I feel – and the overall health and wellness of my journey. I was happy and healthy, and it wasn't based on the number that I was seeing on the scale, or the weight that I thought I needed to be at.

As I continued with my journey, that number on the scale kept staring at me each week, but I found that it didn't have my full focus like it once did. It wasn't my main goal anymore to see a specific number, especially after the 100-pound mark. There came a point where the number stayed the same and didn't budge for weeks, but this wasn't important to me anymore. I wasn't a failure just because more weight wasn't coming off.

The real work was about to come with what I was going to do next. I created a list of "non-scale victories and goals," like wanting to run 5KM and trying out new activities. These were achievements I once felt like I couldn't accomplish in my lifetime, but I was becoming aware that the scale didn't tell me what my body could do physically.

Although the number on the scale hadn't changed, the size of my clothing drastically changed from an 18 to an 8. I felt confident enough to wear a two-piece swimsuit! The scale didn't tell me how I would love running and would become an avid hiker.

These "non-scale victories and goals" have been more important and impactful to my journey than the number on the scale, although it took a while for me to realize that. I wish I knew this when I stepped onto the scale and saw the 257 pounds "yelling" at me. I was programmed to base my success on the number of pounds that I lost. If the number of the scale decreased, I considered it to be a good week; if it increased, I saw it as a bad week and was hard on myself. Thankfully, that has changed. My mindset has now shifted to thinking that a "good week" is when I accomplish something, try something new for the first time, or maybe go out of my comfort zone. I have also discarded the word "bad week" from my vocabulary.

Usually, stress and other life challenges contribute more to those types of feelings than food and activity.

I started to realize that if I treated myself to a donut or a beer one day, that didn't make or break my journey or the number on the scale. In fact, it was starting to feel healthier to me that I wasn't restricting myself, per my new lifestyle. The scale shows a number that has been programmed in our brains to be the most important aspect of how to feel about ourselves**. I am here to tell you that it is just a number!** That number can change for many reasons: hormones, menstrual cycles, medication, stress, muscle changes, and so on. It is not just about what we eat. **The number on the scale does not represent your worth, nor does it fully reflect your progress through your wellness journey.**

I often still struggle with my body, and I don't always feel positive about what I see. It isn't something that comes easily to me, and that is perfectly okay. I have come to accept that. This body is mine, and it's here to stay with me for life. I accept all the bumps, bruises, marks, and discolorations. My body offers me so much more than the appearance.

Here is another story to share about my mindset shift and how I handled new adventures:

I was at a waterpark with Josh, and we wanted to go down the tube slide (What? Me going down a tube slide? Like, WHAT?). When we got the tube, I saw a sign that read, "maximum weight 400 pounds, scale at the top and will weigh you and turn you away if you don't meet the guidelines," or something along those lines. My heart started beating. Josh weighed about 210 pounds at the time, which meant that I had to be 190 pounds or less to go on this ride. Was I going to fall under this weight limit? When we got to the top, I noticed there were a couple of girls behind us who were 14 or 15 years old. They were talking about how they need to get weighed at the top. We get up to the top and the attendant says, "Okay, I need you to step on the scale." Josh went first, weighed in at 195 pounds, and said, "yes, I lost 15 pounds since the last time I weighed myself." Then, it was my turn. My heart was still thumping in my chest. I got on the scale and I weighed 183 pounds. I said, with confidence, "WOW, 5 pounds up from last time, yes!" I turned to look at the two girls, and they looked puzzled by my response. Then, I said to Josh, "Now, let's go on this tube, Honey."

My mindset was, yes, the number "said something" but it didn't mean anything to me. I felt like a kid going down a water tube slide, and it was fucking amazing, because I had turned the experience into a positive, despite a small increase on the scale. It's moments like these that I celebrate and embrace.

Since then, I focus on living in the moment, enjoying all of the moments, and really embracing what my body gives me. I wore that swimsuit with pride when I went down the slide, and I enjoyed my time. I am so thankful. I don't worry if people see my skin tags or if my rolls are out. I enjoy my body and its ability to go down a slide like a 10-year-old!

Recently, when a friend of mine asked if I wanted a bag of clothes that she was getting rid of, my first thought was, *I will never fit into those; she is so tiny.* Well, my friends, I DID FIT INTO THOSE SMALL CLOTHES. I put the clothes on, smiled, and cried at the same time. This was the feeling; this was another "a-ha moment." It felt far more impactful than a few weeks ago when I stepped on that damn scale to see that I had lost 100 pounds. THIS is what made this journey and effort worth it for me. Also, to note, I had gained about 12 pounds back at this point, so I was no longer "100 pounds lighter." I wasn't at the goal weight that I had in mind from the start, yet I was the happiest, strongest, and most confident that I have ever been as I stood there wearing the clothing and weighing approximately 169 pounds. To me, these are the moments that I am most proud of. The work I put into myself and my wellness journey wasn't just to lose 100 pounds, it was also to gain that confidence and self-love, to really appreciate my body for what it gives me: strength, self- esteem, happiness, and love. I finally loved what I saw. I felt beautiful, worthy, and just fucking awesome.

I have come a long way since I started my journey. I would say that my mind-set shift has had the biggest impact on me. I went from being embarrassed with my appearance, worrying about what others thought of me, and feeling sluggish and tired all the time, to really focusing on what I was eating, the activities that made me feel better each day, and embracing and being proud of my accomplishments along the way. I soon learned that my mind needed more work than my body, and yet it took longer for me to realize it. Now, I feel comfortable and confident in situations and I have control over how I react. Simple things don't feel like a huge task or worry anymore.

I am no longer a bystander at Josh's family cottage. I have gone from hiding behind oversized t-shirts five years ago, to wearing a two-piece swimsuit and paddle boarding with strength and self-confidence. I also now kayak, swim as much as I can, and participate in the fun activities.

Oh, and did I mention that I was also riding a tube on the back of a boat? I would have never done these activities before, because my mind was telling me that I couldn't. My body was ready and eager, but I just didn't have the confidence I needed. I don't let anything come in my way now. I believe in myself, and I don't let negative thoughts takeover. *Jill, your rolls will show. Jill, your cellulite! Jill, you're showing too much skin.* Nope, not today, negative thoughts! Yes, all of that is showing, and I am proud of my body for being active and beautiful each day. When I participate in physical activities that my body is craving, I feel much more confident in my body, especially if my mind had initially made me doubt myself. I can, and I will, continue to do hard things.

I share my story with you because I know that many women struggle with feeling confident and pretty, no matter their size. And I am here to tell you: you are worthy. Your body size and weight do not matter and will not make you less of a person. Focusing on getting to my end "goal," which was a number, was programmed into my mind for so long. When I finally looked at my health as a whole, I felt so much better about myself – both mentally and physically. I felt comfortable in my skin and started really loving myself and every aspect of my wellness journey.

## I AM HERE TO TELL YOU: YOU ARE WORTHY!

Your worth is from within. It's from the memories you make and the life you live. It's the feelings around you that make you YOU, not your swimsuit, or pants size, or the scale number. We are programmed to think that the damn number on the scale is equal to our worth. When my focus shifted and I started feeling valid in my skin and appreciating what my body gives me and is doing for me, I started feeling confident and empowered, no matter the size or weight I was.

Your body is a lot more powerful than your mind, and I have learned to listen to my body rather than what I think my mind is trying to tell me. The reality is that the number 257 isn't scary, but neither is 183; they are both just numbers. Go out and swim, get on that paddleboard, start training to run a 5KM, or whatever it is that you have always thought you could never do. Try it! You will be surprised that your body can go against your mind and do hard things to achieve whatever is outside of your normal routine or comfort zone.

I wish I knew when I first started that the number on the scale does not determine my worth. *You are worthy, Jill, no matter your size or weight. Your outer shell does not determine your inner worth.* This is the truth, and now I live this everyday. I am confident, comfortable, and happy with my body the way it is. I embrace all of myself, inside and out.

But really, friends, I am just your average Jill, learning how to become a stronger, healthier, and happier version of myself each day. Everyone's journey is very different, so **be YOU, do YOU, and appreciate YOU**. You are worthy, and your voice is worth being heard. And if I can suggest one thing: just throw out that damn scale!

I DON'T NEED TO APOLOGIZE FOR THE PERSON I AM TODAY; THERE IS NOTHING "WRONG" WITH ME, EVEN AT A WEIGHT THAT I MAY NOT BE THRILLED *with.*

# *Chapter 10*

# JOANNA MENEZES

AUTHOR PHOTO: ANNYA MILLER PHOTOGRAPHY
joannamenezes0923@gmail.com

I was fourteen years old when I went on my first official "diet"...14! You know, one of those ones that was super popular in the 90s, where you go and get weighed in every week, buy pre-packaged meals and snacks that cost a fortune, and then they either cheer or wag their finger at you based on how much weight you lost, or didn't lose? I was so young that my mother had to sign a waiver saying that she gave permission for me to participate in the program, which she did, because I had all but begged her to. Like most 14 year olds, I thought I knew everything when I didn't really know very much at all. However, what I did know was that the body I was in was not good enough and it needed to change. My search for unwavering perfection began earlier than that, I am sure, but this was definitely a defining moment in my life.

Hi there, I'm Joanna. I am the youngest of three siblings and come from a long line of strong, responsible, Sicilian women. Being a true helper and empath in every sense of the word, it isn't surprising that I pursued a career in education. Since I always strive for more in life, my background in education eventually led me to becoming a small business owner in the supplemental education field. I am also the mother of two amazing teenage boys and have been married to the most supportive man for 21 years.

My struggles with weight loss and self-worth have coloured each of these relationships in very different ways. My striving to always be everything to everyone as a daughter, sister, wife, mother, and boss has brought me here. My hope is that this chapter will help just one person feel seen and heard – even if that one person is only me.

## I ALMOST DIDN'T WRITE THIS CHAPTER, BECAUSE I'M NOT COOL ENOUGH!

Early in 2021, I was working with an absolutely wonderful personal coach whom I will refer to only as "K.K." when the opportunity to work on this project came about. She was supporting me and a group of other amazing women in being able to identify what success meant to us. One of the activities that she had us do was to write down our goals for the next six months as successes that had already happened. On my list of six month successes was that I had started writing a book. Within a few days, the lead author of this book posted the opportunity for women to join her project. Cue the goosebumps! I ignored that first post, but it kept popping up louder and louder every time, until I could no longer ignore it. At the last minute, I submitted my application and was accepted. Cue the nausea!

My next instinct was to reach out to K.K. and tell her what I had done and have her talk me off the ledge that I was precariously perched upon. After all, so many of the other women seemed to have these amazing careers and stories and strong personalities with awesome social media presence. I was just me. The only pictures on my social media accounts are of me and my family, and even those are sparse. I don't do "Reels" or "Lives" or "Tik Toks." I don't have a large following of people who are going to pre-order this book. Maybe I had made a mistake in applying. Perhaps the universe was not telling me what I thought it was telling me. Perhaps the universe was just telling me to stop dreaming and come back down to earth. K.K. is normally the master of helping me come to my own conclusions, but in this case she quite simply said, "you have to do this." So here I am, because in my own way, I am cool enough!

# I ALMOST DIDN'T WRITE THIS CHAPTER, BECAUSE DON'T I ALREADY HAVE ENOUGH TO DO?

Life is hard. Being a mom to teenage boys is fucking hard. Running a brick and mortar business with employees who depend on you through a pandemic is REALLY fucking hard! The pandemic was challenging for everyone for very different reasons. In addition to having the constant concerns for the health and safety of my immediate family and elderly parents, I had the added stress of having a business completely shut down by the pandemic in March of 2020. My whole business model had to "pivot" (I hate that word now) to an online format.

Let me explain a bit. I work with students of all ages who, for one reason or another, have fallen behind at school. They are struggling readers. They have low confidence. They have challenges with focus. They have identified learning disabilities, and the list goes on. These are students who need the support we offer in the manner in which we offer it. They are not the kind of children who will do well with online learning. But what choice did we have? I was dead set against it. I was going to ride out this two-week shutdown and then get everyone back in-person where they belonged.

After the first week, I quickly realized that this was going to be longer and far worse than any of us initially believed, so I put on my big girl pants and moved my staff and students online. However, my people pleasing side took over and when I made that move to online (that I did not believe for a second was going to be successful), I felt terribly guilty charging parents for a service that I was not confident with. So I charged them half the normal amount for that first month. Parents were grateful since they were also dealing with so many unknowns. I was happy that I had dealt with the situation with kindness and integrity. I was also terrified at the loss of revenue and needing to feed my own family.

Many would say that this kindness is my greatest weakness. Sometimes I agree with them. Sometimes I wish I was a bigger bitch. The rest of the time, I am proud that I can empathize with others and that I can sleep at night knowing that I have handled an impossible situation with grace and honesty.

I still lost forty percent of my enrollment and revenue in April of 2020, despite my kindness. I still continued to maintain a brick and mortar location through months and months of shut downs. I quickly ate through my savings for the "rainy day" that became a monsoon. I also quickly ate my way through a lot of cookies, chips, ice cream, and pasta!

Endless days of sitting in front of a screen to try and keep my business alive and also work with the students I had left led to a non-existent movement routine. Let's face it; the only exercise that I was getting was in lifting food to my mouth and clicking on the keyboard! The "COVID 15" would have been a blessing for me. My weight gain was more like the "COVID 40."

My entire life was out of control and I had no idea where to start to rebuild it. More importantly, I had no desire to rebuild it. I was going through the motions of running my business. I was going through the motions of being a wife and mother. I was simply existing and surviving. I felt that I had no one to turn to because I believed that no one would have any clue what I was going through or how to help.

I felt defeated and alone, like I have through most of my life challenges. The only comfort that I had was food. After all, everyone was stress eating due to the pandemic, so that gave me permission to as well, right?

The overwhelm of the last year-and-a-half has only heightened my struggles with body image and self-worth. The only difference is that this time, I am actively looking for ways to accept where I am and show myself the same kindness, tolerance, and patience that I show to everyone else in my life. So that's why *I HAD* to make time to write this chapter, even though I already had enough to do.

## I ALMOST DIDN'T WRITE THIS CHAPTER, BECAUSE IT MIGHT NOT BE PERFECT.

"Am I good enough?" This is a question every woman asks herself at some point (or maybe several points) in her life. Of course you are good enough! In fact, you are perfect! If you're not perfect, you better figure out how to fake it until you are! Don't do anything to "make people talk." In a traditional Sicilian family, what that really means is don't disappoint your parents. So, growing up, I did everything right. *I STILL* do everything right – ALL THE TIME! The pressure of that is enough to make anyone eat their body weight in lasagna and fresh cannoli! While high parental expectations are not unique to my family or culture, when you are the person on the inside, you truly feel like your situation is worse than anyone else's.

Despite always doing the "right thing," marrying the "right man," living in the "right house," raising the "right kids," and planning for the "right future," there is always a voice in my head reminding me that it is still not enough. I am not by any means complaining about my life. I am so grateful for the world I immediately live in, but the voices of my traditional Sicilian parents will forever dictate the path my life takes.

My parents are amazing. They truly are. My father worked 80 hours a week while my mother stayed home and took care of the kids and the house and her aging mother and, and, and. They gave us a good life. We had a beautiful home to live in. We were fed, healthy, and loved. Our university education was paid for. Our weddings were paid for. Our own children are loved by them, beyond measure. All that they ask for in return is respect, and for us to "do the right thing" – is that such a terrible expectation? Likely not for the average person, but for me, it can be crippling. This expectation makes me put unbelievable amounts of pressure on myself to make sure that everything is perfect. My house is perfectly clean even though I am exhausted with a business and two kids. My business is running perfectly, even though I am literally dragging it through one of the worst times in our lives. My kids need to be getting perfect grades, because being in the education sector, what kind of mother would I be if they weren't? My marriage needs to be perfect, even if it only appears that way to everyone looking in, because marriage is also fucking hard!

This image of perfection that I try to maintain daily certainly does not help with my struggles with body image and weight. Eat behind closed doors, at night when no one can see you but your husband. A husband who loves you so much that he will do whatever you think you need, whether that means joining you on your latest workout kick or bringing you chips to eat while watching TV at night (because he knows that you are exhausted and stressed and chips make you happy). At least in the moment they do. Some might say he is enabling me. I say that he is just trying to do his best to navigate through a life full of stress with a wife who is not necessarily open about her emotions. He takes two cues from me that tell him when I've hit my limit. Either I don't speak at all, or I sob uncontrollably. There is no in between, and he handles it all with the strength that every woman wishes for in a partner. The way I handle stress is totally on me, not on him. He's just the poor, kind soul going through it with me.

I absolutely do not always say and do the right things. I am sure that I am not saying all of the right things right now. Expecting to be perfect at breaking perfectionist habits really is quite the oxymoron! Hopefully the things I am saying are perfect enough to resonate with some other off-the-charts-

Type-A perfectionists out there, and we can all come to the realization that breaking the habits that we've used throughout our existence takes time.

## I ALMOST DIDN'T WRITE THIS CHAPTER, BECAUSE I'M 'THE STRONG ONE.'

I feel like every member of a family takes on a "role" in their family in order to keep things moving forward. In my own personal circles, anyway, every family has a sibling who thrives on drama, a sibling who is the "strong one," a parent who is the "strict one," and a parent who is the "pushover," and the list goes on and on. Each family dynamic creates the roles that it needs to survive.

Any guesses as to which role is mine? Yup, "the strong one." Even though it has never been officially assigned, I took on the role of being the "strong one" who did everything right at an early age. It probably occurred around the time that I went on that first diet and was suddenly not the "chubby" one in the family anymore. Did I always feel loved as a child? Of course. But did I feel *more* loved by family and friends after I had lost 30 pounds? Absolutely. It wasn't intentional and it wasn't outwardly expressed to me, but the more positive attention and comments that I got after losing the weight definitely showed me that now that there was "less of me," there was more of me to love. Pretty heavy stuff for a teenager to internalize and then carry with her forever.

Not long after that first diet, there was a pretty substantial life event caused by the "dramatic one" in our family dynamic. I was now 16, and, without going into great detail, this substantial shift caused my parents great heartache. Watching them go through that caused me to immediately decide that I needed to make sure that I NEVER did anything to hurt them like that, EVER! I never wanted to be the cause of seeing pain on their faces like that again. No way, no how. I was going to be the strong one who kept going for them. Never mind how I was feeling; they needed me to be "good."

Don't forget, I was also going through sadness dealing with what had happened, but I could not show that to them because they had "enough to deal with."

So I kept going. I kept being a good student. I kept being a good daughter. I kept helping out at home. I kept being the one everyone could rely on. I kept everything inside. I kept the weight off, but not for very long. That was the start of emotional eating for me. Prior to that, I had been the chubby kid who just wasn't losing the baby weight like everyone else. Now I was beginning my cycle of stress eating and pretending I was fine, eating my feelings and slowly gaining the weight back.

There were a couple more occurrences of drama by this particular member of our cast over the next few years. Every time, my role as the strong one held fast, but my resentment for this role grew stronger. Soon, eating and gaining weight became my way of getting back at everyone for not seeing that I was also struggling and hurt.

Those last few years in high school and then university should have been the best years of my life, but instead they were riddled with drama and upset. I met my now husband when I was 18 and we had some really great friends whom we are still close with to this day. Our foursome was my lifeline. Unfortunately, that lifeline also came with an increased reliance on food to hide the pain behind my smile. It didn't happen quickly, by any means. It was a slow progression. A few pounds here and there over the next eight years until I got married, and I finally felt like I could breathe and be myself, except I didn't know who "myself" was.

I had gone from my father's house to my husband's house and I had no idea who I was as an individual. I had never had the time to think about who I was or who I wanted to be because I was so busy being everything to everybody else. So now it was even more critical to keep up the facade and to hide how truly NOT put together I was out of fear of being judged. Food never judged me… and then the weight packed on.

Being married gave me a comfort zone that I never had before. My husband still is – and always will be – my comfort zone. I am forever grateful for that comfort zone, but I've realized that this comfort zone has become my excuse for not living my best life. This comfort zone has been the place where I buried all of my resentment from past life experience and simply started going through the motions of my life – not at all because my husband has imposed that upon me, but because he made me feel so loved that I thought none of that stuff mattered anymore.

I see now that that "stuff" has made me who I am – the good and the bad. I see now that recognizing the "stuff" and actively choosing to not have that in my life anymore is what is going to help me move forward in my journey. I don't want to be "the strong one" anymore – and that's a choice that I am allowed to make.

I am accepting myself for who I am and how I came to be here. I am a pretty amazing wife, mother, business owner, and friend. **I don't need to apologize for the person I am today; there is NOTHING "wrong" with me, even at a weight that I may not be thrilled with.** Not all of the things that happened in my life were of my choosing, but the roles I took on because of those experiences were choices that I made based on the stories I was telling myself at the time – and continue to tell myself to this day. That's the great thing about choices, though; you can always make new ones and write a new story.

## I ALMOST DIDN'T WRITE THIS CHAPTER, BECAUSE I FEEL LIKE A FRAUD.

Fake, fraud, impostor, phony, flimflammer (that last one is my favorite)! No matter which word you choose, they all describe how I felt while writing this chapter. What do I know about achieving body bliss? I am a living example of being on one failed diet after another. One failed exercise program after another. One failed attempt at personal growth after another. I have nothing to offer! I have no gleaming insights to share with people that will bring them ultimate success in their journey towards weight loss and body acceptance! Or do I?

I lost a bunch of weight again back in 2017. I woke up one day and decided that I was tired of feeling tired. I was at a point in my life where my kids were grown enough and my business was solid enough that I could start to take care of me.

I didn't do anything crazy. I just started making better food choices and walking every day. I didn't deprive myself of anything because I knew that deprivation would make me want it more. So if I wanted a cookie, I ate it. If I wanted some chips, I ate them. For some reason, I had this newfound willpower and drive that moved me away from eating the whole bag of chips and toward a healthier relationship with food. It was working! I was slowly and steadily losing weight and gaining more energy. I had made a "lifestyle change" that was great! (Until it wasn't.)

After about six months, the scale stopped moving. I had lost almost 30 pounds on my own without drastic measures and now it wasn't working anymore. I was trying everything to break this "plateau" and nothing was working. I was determined this time to not give up on this new way of living, so I hired a personal trainer. She came to my home twice a week and pushed me to do exercises that I had never heard of and never thought that

I could do. It was great and I was getting stronger. After the first month, I had lost a crapload of inches, but the scale still was not moving.

I persisted with this for another year. This time, with no movement on the scale and no movement in inches lost, either. Why was I bothering? The increased energy that I had gained at the start of this once-successful journey was dwindling and those thoughts came creeping back in again. I was upset and stressed – this time not because of my life circumstances, but because I was successful at losing weight, and then I wasn't anymore. Even though I was doing "everything right" (there she is again, the one who does everything right). I thought that losing more weight was the answer to happiness, so I *needed* it to happen. And maybe if it wasn't happening, it was because I didn't *deserve* to be happy.

So here we were in 2019 – and I gave up. I decided that if eating well and working out almost daily wasn't working, then I was just going to eat what I wanted and exercise if I felt like it and just see what happened.

Again, the weight slowly came back, but it wasn't drastic enough to propel me into action to stop it from getting any worse. Before I knew it, it was March 2020 and the world as we knew it changed. That's when the weight packed back on for the umpteenth time – and that's also when I realized that my struggles with weight and body image were about more than just bad food choices and a lack of motivation. This is a constant journey and an endless learning process. The ups and downs are part of the process.

I now understand that my lack of the ideal prescription for success is exactly the thing that I have to offer. It's okay if you feel like you are taking one step forward and seventeen back. I do this daily! What I am learning along the way is to take different steps back and to make sure that the one step forward that I do take each day is a solid one based on learning, growth, and love.  Sometimes I still feel like a flimflammer, but a more enlightened one!

## I ALMOST DIDN'T FINISH THIS CHAPTER.

This was not an easy task for me. The words did not come effortlessly. In fact, they kind of came all at once and almost at the last minute! I kept procrastinating. I kept thinking about backing out. I kept telling myself that there was no way that I was going to finish it. All of my life, the stories I told myself revolved around making sure that I did not let anyone down. Remember my Sicilian background...we don't disappoint because then "people will talk." You know what? I don't care about what people think anymore (okay, I kind of do, but I care a little less than before – and that's progress)! I realized that if I didn't finish writing this chapter, I would be letting myself down. And if it has never been okay for me to let other people down, then it sure as shit wasn't going to be okay for me to let myself down!

I rarely do things for myself. Finally making myself and my goals a priority was the next essential step along this path of forgiveness and acceptance. Sharing my story was not selfish or egotistical. It was the first true act of kindness that I have ever shown myself. My hope is that in this chapter, someone out there now knows that they are not alone.

A person is not defined by whether they have met childhood expectations – self-imposed or not. Everyone deserves to be happy right now, the way they are. Leave the guilt, take the cannoli (that's a spin on a "Godfather" reference for my friends in the back)!

I FINALLY WROTE THIS CHAPTER, AND I AM SO GLAD THAT I DID.

# Chapter 11

# LYN HOUSSER

AUTHOR PHOTO: PHOTOGRAPHY BEITZ
IG: @coach_muffin

*I am a personal trainer and owner of Coach Muffin Personal Training. My journey to loving my body and being has taken time, hard work, and learning to trust myself. As a mom and a wellness professional, I strive to be raw and authentic in all that I do – and I hope that this approach can create real change in the world!*

Bodies are so very complicated, with so many systems and parts that affect one another. The only thing more complicated than our bodies themselves, is the narrative created about them. There are so many intricate bits and pieces. Many words, looks, and subtle things (and sometimes not-so-subtle things) lead us to believe this narrative is our truth, when so often it starts with the words and actions of others. The power, impact, and weight they have the potential to carry is immense and can last a lifetime.

As a child, my world was filled with people who saw a woman as simply someone whose role was defined by being a submissive partner and their ability to bear healthy children. Bodies were not to be considered "sexy."

Girls were shamed for attracting attention or wearing certain things. I can remember an uncle telling my family at Christmas that I looked like a slut. I was twelve and my floor length skirt had a slit that went up to my knees. Female bodies shouldn't be faster or stronger than men. Voices shouldn't be too loud. Opinions couldn't be different. Don't question anything. Apologize profusely. You must never say "no" to an adult, and as a woman, you couldn't pray or speak during church.

I watched my mother weigh herself frequently and I can remember the words so clearly – and the power that those words held over her. The adults would discuss the latest fad diets…the shakes and cabbage soup, which would then become a part of our home for a brief period. I heard the words about my body even then. "Oh, Lyn's so skinny! What a scrawny kid! Such knobby knees. Frog legs. Toothpick arms."

When I look back, I can't pick the moment where those words changed me. I can't remember the moment in time when I lost that carefree little girl with her long auburn hair, but it happened. I lost the desire to try new things. I didn't attempt anything that I thought I couldn't master right away. I wouldn't speak up and I tried to become as invisible as possible. My voice almost ceased to exist.

As I moved into high school, that voice became harder to find. I'd throw up before presentations or stay home "sick" because sometimes that meant I could just present to a teacher the next day. Gym classes brought so many excuses when needed – a sore wrist or my asthma – whatever it took to not feel singled out.

I remember a teacher asking why I wasn't going to try out for field hockey in grade 9. I couldn't even understand why she would suggest that. Didn't she hear what other people were saying in high school? "Wow, Lyn, I could snap you in half! Look at your little arms! Eww your boobs are so small. Just so weak!" Someone followed me into the bathroom to see if I was bulimic, so I stopped using the washroom during the school day. I continued to try to stay in the shadows and remain unseen.

My big win was deciding to apply to college, despite being told there was no point. My job was to find a husband and make babies, but I did it anyway. I packed up and moved four hours away. I specifically chose a school that would allow me space and a new beginning.

College brought my first boyfriend and that shit got serious fast! He was controlling, jealous, and his temper flared easily and often. He began isolating me from my friends early on. I did try ending it once but was threatened and hurt. There were so many tears, but the pressure from my family was to marry quickly. That's what good girls do. My friends tried talking me out of it but my upbringing and lack of confidence had me convinced that any red flags were probably my fault. The words that I heard reinforced the fact that I wasn't good enough. A month after graduating college, I was married. I had just turned twenty years old.

The words turned into sharper knives. If there was a way to hurt me with words, he'd find it and use it. My intelligence, body, work ethic, cooking, friends, family, education, job, tastes...they were all fair game. I was weak, stupid, and "lucky that he married me" when I looked the way I looked. From words, it progressed. The bank account would be drained regularly. Sex wasn't an option. Saying no just meant the sheets would be bloodier and my body was going to be in pain. The isolation worsened. Time with my friends became non-existent. I was gently removed from a bridal party. I went to family things alone or found a reason to not be able to be there. I walked on eggshells most of the time.

A positive pregnancy test brought anger, and I lost the baby alone on the bathroom floor.

A few years later, I was pregnant again. His anger still being taken out on my body, I called my dad sobbing one day because I was bleeding and terrified. I didn't lose the baby and went back to working 60 hours a week to pay our bills. That baby girl arrived 7 weeks early and it became obvious within those first 48 hours that her journey was more complicated than that of a preemie. She was rushed to the neonatal intensive care unit and it was hours before I could see her. As I went to have a shower, my husband requested that I step on the scale. On the most traumatizing day of my life, he wanted to know if I could fit back into my jeans.

For the next seven weeks, that baby girl fought with everything she had. Doctors told me to start planning her funeral. I spent the entire time with her. 10:00 a.m. to 11:00 p.m. everyday. Back to Ronald Mcdonald House for some sleep, food, and to pump. It felt like Groundhog Day, but there was no quitting. I needed her to make it. He'd show up about once a week. A short visit with her and then I knew what was expected of me. She was 5 days old and my body was attempting to heal. The social worker at RMH sat me down because she watched me carry bloody sheets out of my room. I covered for him, as always. An incident involving him screaming at me in front of the hospital staff and threatening to take my baby away had the hospital social workers sitting down with me multiple times. Hearing someone say that I was a failure as a mother because "you couldn't even keep that baby from coming early" stung. God did those words hurt.

The day that I could bring that baby home terrified me. I walked out of the hospital alone with a five-pound baby. His handgun shoot took precedence. I was humiliated, struggling into the elevator with all of our things alone. It was hard to watch dads opening doors and gently helping their partners into cars. My drive home took twice as long as I kept pulling over to check on her. Home should've felt safe, but I walked into mountains of laundry and dishes, bathrooms that needed cleaning, and garbages that were overflowing. An empty fridge and a husband who walked in expecting me to cook dinner. He greeted me with, "What kind of wife are you?"

A baby in the house meant new ways to abuse me. Attacking my parenting became an easy target. If I needed a break from the baby who barely slept, I obviously couldn't handle motherhood. The bank account would be emptied as I'd get ready to spend yet another day at a specialist appointment. Again, alone. Out of over 400 appointments in her twelve years of life, he made it to one. I was also pumping to feed her every two hours and maintaining a house. He continued to play his sports and pursue his hobbies. I cut grass and shoveled snow. If supper was late or wasn't what he wanted, all hell would break loose. Not having started the dryer one night had him tossing me and the mattress out of bed early one morning.

I was the closest to breaking as I've ever been. Heading back to work, I tried hiding it from my coworkers. I talked to clients about healthy relationships, boundaries, and abuse. I couldn't imagine the failure my coworkers would think I was if they knew what I was living through.

My life changed the day my coworker, Tash, said that she wanted to train to run 5km. We weren't close and it sounded terrifying, but I asked if I could join her. Three days a week were devoted to training and it was so hard. My asthma and self-doubt nagged me through those 30 minutes each time. His words continued to attack my strength, but I kept going. Tash and I kept telling ourselves "one more fencepost."

That sweet baby was tucked in the stroller feeding snacks to Tash's dog while we ran. Our conversations quickly became deep and I started talking. She didn't judge and I finally felt seen. The space while running was sacred and safe. I reached out to someone in his family to see if they could offer some insight and was told to be glad he wasn't hitting me in my face. This alone was proof he loved me because visible marks on my face would've let others know I needed to do better as a wife.

I suggested counseling and he agreed, providing that it was his minister. When I spilled my guts in our first session, I used the world "rape." The minister informed me that there is no such thing as rape in a marriage. I had a duty as a wife and saying no was not allowed. His advice? Pray to become a better wife. Ask to have a better understanding of what it means to be submissive and holy. I should also start spending time with "godly" couples in their church to start mentoring me in the ways that I could be the wife he deserved.

Going to see my family doctor during this time also had him being very blunt with me. His exam showed scar tissue and damage caused by my husband's anger. The doctor's words were unforgettable and impactful. "Lyn, you weigh 92 pounds and have the blood pressure of an extremely overweight 70-year-old man. If he doesn't kill you with his bare hands, he will kill you through stress."

Shortly after, Tash and I ran our hardest training run yet and I remember her asking me what my next goal was. I blurted out instantly, "I need to get a divorce and get out!" I had this sudden realization that if he was okay treating me this way, our daughter wouldn't be safe from his temper or words, either.

Leaving meant forming a safety plan. My employer was informed. I had someone lined up to be with me for safety when I told him, and I felt good about the plan. That day didn't go like it was written on paper. He saw my dad in town with a moving truck the day before and our timeline moved up. I told him at a public park that night and was told to show up in the morning and get my things. When I arrived, he kicked my sister off the property. I am eternally grateful that she heard the click of the deadbolt and called 911 as soon as she walked away. Inside the house, his anger was almost indescribable. My cell phone started ringing and I remember him yelling at me to ignore it. "Your meddling friends, I bet!" When I didn't answer, the landline started to ring and the display read "OPP dispatch." He answered and told the dispatcher that everything was fine. We were simply having a conversation. The saint of a dispatcher insisted he hand me the phone. As soon as she heard my voice, she said "we're a few minutes out but

I need your help. Give me yes or no answers but not details."

"Is your daughter in the room with you?"
"Yes."

"Are there firearms in the house?"
"Yes."

"Does he have the keys to the gun safe on him?"
"Yes."

"Is he close to the gun safe right now?"
"Yes."

"When I say go, be ready to cover your daughter's body with yours and stay low. No matter what. We need to keep that baby safe. You can do this mama." Those were the words I needed. They grounded and reassured me in that moment, but also in so many others later on in life. My grandma Thelma used to say, "Spring always follows winter. It hasn't failed us yet." This is something that I didn't understand the value of in those childhood moments, but it resonates so deeply now.

**

We started our new life and running was still a big part of it. It was still that sacred, safe space and I used it as I began to process and heal. When I'd feel a panic attack welling up, I'd grab my shoes and the running stroller. I signed up for my first 5km obstacle course race and felt invincible. I did another and then decided that I needed to do something bigger – and quite impulsively came to the conclusion that I was going to run 108km from "my" Ronald McDonald House in London to where I lived in Listowel. It was an opportunity to give back.

I joined a gym and started to strength train for the first time ever. Honestly, that part scared me more than the actual running. The women at the gym seemed to know what they were doing. Their outfits coordinated perfectly, they had cute ponytails, gym bags, and playlists… it was all scary as hell, but this big goal was going to require 6 days a week at the gym. The more time that I spent in the gym, the more comfortable I became. The words of encouragement started to be spoken – first internally, and then I slowly started to say them out loud. My words truly had power!

I completed my 108km of painful, enlightening, and empowering miles. Miles that proved how strong I truly was. I began to see the beauty that could come from taking chances and not being afraid. Facing my own fears began changing every aspect of my life. I changed careers and became a trainer. I had another baby (which was a thought that had terrified me. I was then blessed with the most mini version of myself that could've ever been made). I left a relationship. I outgrew friendships. I started sharing my story and using the power of my own words – words that strengthened me but were suddenly also providing strength to others. Words spoken while training clients. Words that were shared in a magazine article. Words that became resources at women's retreats. Well-placed words in yoga classes and coaching calls. Raw words. Real words.

Opportunities in fitness can be tough. So much of the emphasis is placed on appearance and it becomes very easy for self-doubt to pop in. Sometimes those words from the past creep in. What about my little boobs or biceps that aren't bulging? What about the days when my abs don't pop? The more I asked for feedback from clients and people I respected, the clearer it became. My value and worth didn't come from my body. Wellness is so much more than the glossy covers of magazines! It's about learning to appreciate the body you have at this moment. A body that's taken you through this journey with the traumas and trials. It's worthy of celebration. This body might have acne scars, stretch marks, and butt dimples, but this body is strong! This woman is fierce!

A quiet leader. An active community builder. A cheerleader. A listener. An empath. A voice. A mentor. A teacher. An advocate. A coach. A friend. A mama. A learner. A connector of people. An athlete. *A survivor.* Words that help reinforce where my true value lies. Am I being a human who is kind? What do I need from my body to bring me happiness? Can it carry me on all the adventures I plan to take?

Last weekend, I spent two days at Blue Mountain for the Spartan OCR race weekend. A torn ligament eight weeks earlier meant that all of my training meant nothing for this event. My two days of competition couldn't happen. Being bitter would've been easy, but I went up anyway. As I watched the sun come up over the water from my perch up the mountain, I was overwhelmed with so much gratitude.

A wave of gratitude that swept over the entire weekend. Volunteering meant that I was immersed in one of my communities. It gave me a chance to be that encourager and cheerleader (Who had 100% of the 1100 racers complete the A Frame climb). My empathic nature, coaching, and quiet leadership skills calmed nervous athletes. My ankle wasn't strong enough to run, but my body handled a 15-hour volunteer shift. I came away with knowledge, new skills, and some amazing friendships. It meant watching my clients race and prove something to themselves. Standing on that mountain realizing that I had raced my first OCR race 10 years prior, I was blown away by this woman, who was no longer defined by the narrative of others, but by my own damn words!

# Chapter 12

## NICOLE JACKSON

IG: @hnicolejackson

Low carb, high fat. Low fat, high carb. Calorie counting. Measuring portions and weighing every morsel. Eliminating entire food groups.Vegetarian. Paleo. Keto. Meal replacement shakes. Flexitarian. Natural weight loss supplements. Exogenous ketones. Intense exercise. Moderate exercise. Intermittent fasting. Not eating after 7 pm. Vegetable soup before every meal. Huge amounts of water. Green tea. Coffee. No caffeine. Eating nothing white. Eating everything white. Diet foods. Sugar-free foods. I've tried them all. And the one thing they all had in common? I may have lost 10-15 pounds, I felt miserable, my body felt like crap – and I still wasn't satisfied with how my body looked. I was more committed to the scale and my obsession with weight loss than I was to any partner in life. I quite literally obsessed over food continually until finally I had enough.

My name is Nicole. I am a mom, daughter, sister, aunt, and friend. I am also a school principal and yoga teacher. I have a veritable alphabet soup following my name when I choose to use it (and I don't very often!). My greatest accomplishments are my beautiful children, who are amazing people. I drive myself to accomplish more, to achieve more, to be successful. I love animals and have dogs and cats in my life. I love my career; I love the smiling little faces I see every day at school. My yoga students make me smile. I am so proud of all of the growth that I have seen over the years that they've been coming to my classes.

My life is amazing by all counts. I am truly blessed and feel accomplished and successful. All the success in the world, however, does not change the fact that I have a dysfunctional relationship with food. I am a disordered eater with an often tortured and skewed body image – in recovery, I should add. Because recovery isn't in an instant, and no matter how much work you do, there are always those niggling thoughts inching into your mind, around the periphery. Those thoughts and those little jabs at myself are why I consider myself "recovering." Much like an addict, the journey is day-by-day. I'm putting the tools I have learned and are at my disposal to good use.

Let's go back. Way back. Through some intensive work in the past year and a bit, I have made some amazing discoveries. So let's head all the way back to the early 1970s, to a rural community and a little girl with lots of freckles, a turned up button nose, curly hair that her mother kept short to make it manageable, and a natural curiosity that made her what was referred to as "precocious" – which is a nice way to say that she was really bright and drove the adults crazy with her wild and vivid imagination and millions of questions. That adorable little girl was me.

I played and ran barefoot around our home in the country, entertained by the family dog, an imaginary friend named Don, and a groundhog called Mrs. Groundhog. Life was good. We ate lots of vegetables right out of the huge garden that my mom grew. Pop and chips were a treat, only for special occasions. My mom baked the best bran muffins, and with her strawberry jam on top it was the best dessert ever. And the little girl didn't know that her sturdy little legs, wide shoulders, and the natural curve of her little tummy would eventually start the journey down the path of self-hatred, and mistrust of both body and food.

Still quite young, I overheard an adult relative mention to my mother that I was a "sturdy" little girl. I was compared to a cousin, who had a totally different body type and build, more lithe, longer legs, narrow shoulders, and what was considered to be a more attractive appearance to this relative. Those words stuck. I can still hear them all these many years later. Being healthy was not a consideration – that I was genetically blessed with my body type, that made me athletic and a NORMAL young child. I do not recall specifically, but I think there was discussion of watching how many potatoes I ate, and not to allow me to have too much sugar. As if! We ate little sugar at our house, the natural sweetness of fruit being enough.

I know my father was not pleased, and my mother's feelings hurt. At the time, I didn't process what that adult meant, but over the years have come to realize that she meant that I was chubby, even though I was not. This coupled with my mother and grandmother being constantly concerned about weight were the perfect catalyst in a world obsessed with bodies and social norms. I had an aunt, my mother's close sister-in-law, who was always doing one crazy diet or another. It was insane. Watching the women around me who I loved, and emulated, show disdain for their bodies wormed its insidious way into my developing consciousness, and how I viewed health and beauty.

I was always one of the tallest girls in school. Even as a very young girl, I clearly remember not being cool or popular because I had short hair, a nose that was deemed ugly, I was not blonde, and I had a body that was more like the boys. Freckles were just the icing on the ugly cake. And in a sea of Laurie Anns and Kathys, I had a weird name to boot.

Moving through puberty and the teen years – argh. It was painful. Looking back at pictures, I was thin. So thin. Yes, still athletic in build. My swimming kept me muscled and in great shape, but I still had it in my mind that I was chubby. The chubby little girl. I can shake my head at the absurdity of it now. It was painful. I skipped meals. Did not eat so I would not gain weight. I lied about having eaten. I began to binge eventually because I was starving and being active meant I needed the calories. The trading off treats for exercise became a regular occurrence. If I swam x number of lengths, I could have ice cream for a treat, but only if I didn't eat too much at dinner. It wasn't unusual for me to swim a few kilometers, and then go to an hour-long aerobics class in the evening.

Overly sensitive and attuned to every nuance about body size and build, the smallest thing made me harder on myself, and I'd punish myself. I was a growing child. As my body began to mature and curves began to appear, needing a larger size of jeans made me worry that my eating was out of control, that I was fat. I remember in grade 11 or 12, when I had taken to wearing baggy clothes (it was the eighties, perfectly in fashion!), a boy grabbed me and hugged me close. His remark? "You're so skinny under all those clothes!" I know he won't remember, but even though we had been friends since early childhood, I decided then and there that no matter what,

I loved my friend. That remark validated me in a way that I had never experienced. Someone who did not have to love me because I was their child or niece thought I was skinny and liked me for it. Amazing.

Fast-forward to university when the famous "freshman 15" became a part of my reality. Seriously, the poor nutritional choices in the cafeteria coupled with consuming a lot of beer would make any 18 or 19 year old gain weight. Freedom to eat what I wanted, when I wanted, living in Toronto with the vast array and availability of fast food, was like throwing gasoline on a fire. The binging and restriction took on new life, and the wretched hangovers following the late night beer drinking were a boon. Puking my guts up from what was surely close to alcohol poisoning was a good thing! It meant that I was getting rid of calories, and the inability to eat for a day meant that I would cancel out the extra calories and any weight gain. Great attitude, right?

I remember going to a fitness class and almost dying because I was in such poor shape. It shocked me. I was embarrassed to not be able to easily keep up. And my resolve to be skinny got stronger once again. Upon older adult reflection, I can easily see the irony in believing that my state of being unfit simply meant that I was too heavy. Instead of knowing that I needed to engage in exercise to increase my fitness, my resolve was to lose pounds. The diet culture was at the forefront of my mind, and I couldn't see that weight did not mean lacking in fitness. Not doing enough cardiovascular exercise was the issue!

Hot on the heels of university, in fact during my final year of my undergrad, I got pregnant with my first baby. Pregnancy made me adjust and lose some terrible habits. I ate well, walked for fitness, and was very careful not to gain too much pregnancy weight – which, I might add, my doctor emphasized, and which fed what I now recognize as really poor thinking about weight, health, and body image. I endured continual warnings about weight, when I gained just 24 pounds for the entire pregnancy?!

Following pregnancy, I struggled to regain my pre-pregnancy body, which in retrospect was ridiculous. I would never look like a skinny 17-year-old again. I had grown a human in my belly! When you add in breastfeeding and the need for additional calories, dealing with "baby blues" (which I eventually recognized as postpartum depression), zero support with a fussy baby, and a partner who was even more green than I was – why would anyone think that was an ideal time to "bounce back?"

I had an unexpected cesarean section, which ultimately ensured my baby's health. The recovery from surgery alone should alleviate the insane need to look like I did pre-pregnancy! The unrealistic expectations new mothers, and society as a whole, have for postpartum bodies is ridiculous. How about we give ourselves permission to celebrate the little miracles that our bodies grew?

More babies came. I gained more weight. Pictures of my early motherhood years make me sad and embarrassed. I hated myself. Instead of looking at the beautiful children, the challenges faced, and being resilient and surviving, I wish I could erase those years. Not the kids. Never the kids. Me. Erase me. I avoided cameras, and I reflect at times that my children may not ever know they had a mommy who loved them more than life itself. I lost myself and was unrecognizable as that cute wee girl with the upturned nose and sturdy little body. Even now as those beautiful babies are adults, I see fat and desperately unhappy when I look at any pictures that I didn't manage to avoid. It saddens me for myself, but also for all of the other moms who I know feel the same way as I did. It makes me sad for my children. Diet culture essentially robbed them of a happy mommy who would play and be silly because I was obsessing about every morsel of food that I put into my mouth, and I was worried about passing on the fat gene to them.

As an adult, I eventually got skinny, got fat again, got skinny again, and was always on a diet of some kind. I spent a fortune on weight loss. (I wish I had that money in my retirement fund now!). I hope I didn't pass this insanity on to my children, but I know on some level that I did. You don't live with that level of crazy and not pick up on it. I will say that I know I did a pretty good job of talking about being healthy, and using being active as a part of life. My own activity and exercise went through cycles of near obsession, but my kids learned to eat to fuel their bodies. They enjoyed sports, dance, and other activities, and they grew healthy bodies.

During the onset of middle age and the dreaded menopause, my weight again climbed. By this time I had also achieved a high level of career success, and with it, high levels of stress. My mother died of cancer. My father had some health concerns. My marriage ended. One of my children was diagnosed with a life-altering illness. All of these huge stressors worsened my unending cycles of binge eating and eating my emotions – my grief, my sadness, and guilt over my failed marriage (another unhealthy relationship that diminished my sense of self). How the insanity is perpetuated: instead of seeing myself, all that I could see was my dysmorphic body image.

I decided enough was enough. It was time for shit to get real, and for life to be happy. I invested in working with the amazing Dr. Jillian Murphy, ND. I read. I worked on repairing my relationship with food and with my body. I read some more. I was hugely impacted by Sonya Renee Taylor's book, *The Body Is Not An Apology*. I embraced it. My body is not an apology. It is a fucking awesome vessel for my brain, my thoughts, my earthly soul, my entire being. It has birthed babies. It has fed babies. It has run, done a triathlon, done 60 km charity walks more than once. It can swim, keep up with hooligan nephews, and play hard. It can make love, move furniture, walk dogs, kayak, canoe, bike. My body is enough just how it is.

I have moved to the point of declining to be weighed at the doctor. I do not equate my weight or body size to health, and I point out the plethora of peer reviewed studies (yup! I'm that nerdy!) that clearly shows that being over what is considered normal weight by typical health care providers is actually a protective factor. Reading the book "Health At Every Size" by Linda Bacon was a revelation! I have some inherited health stuff like we all do, but it's not because of my weight. I would have those same concerns if I were skeletally thin. When I absolutely need to be weighed (in order to determine the correct dosage amount of medicine, for instance), I bravely step on the scale, eyes closed, and ask that they not tell me the numbers that roll up. I embrace that perimenopausal and menopausal bodies hold fat around the midsection, and honestly, we need to respect the wisdom of Mother Nature. She knows exactly what she's doing! That midsection weight must be some kind of protective factor. Just because modern science cannot explain it does not make it invalid. My body size does not define me as a person or a woman.

I will wear the bikini. Proudly. And not cover it up. And so, the summer of the bikini was born. I am heavier than I would like, if I'm honest. My body is not as muscular or firm as it once was. My skin has lost some of its youthful smoothness. But still, I don my bikini, and spend time at the beach, swimming off the dock, and enjoying the fleeting Canadian summer. Gone are the days of scrambling for a cover up before walking to the washroom, or before having a conversation with someone. If they don't like what they see, they are welcome to avert their eyes because I love what I see – and I could care less!

Wearing a bikini is freeing. It feels great to have an ample amount of skin exposed to the air and sunshine. It is more comfortable than any one-piece bathing suit I've ever owned, has enough support in the top to feel good, and there is no tugging at the bottom because I'm tall and one-piece suits invariably are not quite long enough through the torso. They accommodate my curves and are so comfortable for swimming and playing in the water! One caveat is that I have gone through a lot of sunscreen during the summer of the bikini, but I would have anyway. I need just a bit more to protect delicate skin that has not had as much exposure to the sun's rays. My belly is freckled, beginning to match the rest of my body that is freckled from the years of sunshine warming its skin during summer or on trips to the Caribbean during the bitter Canadian winter.

Part of the freedom of wearing a bikini to enjoy summer fun is the release from the expectations of others. Letting go of that uncomfortable and painful shroud of disapproval and judgment has given me a lightness that I've never experienced before. It's so true that **releasing the weight of the expectations of others is the absolute best weight to lose!** Even when I had starved and exercised myself into thinness, I carried the huge weight of the thoughts and opinions of others on my shoulders. Do others judge me while looking critically at my bare body? Likely. But I don't notice because I'm too busy living my best life. There are zero fucks given about what others think. Really, why do we care? I'm not them. I'm successful, and I have a great life. I don't miss food that I love or a glass of good wine, because I allow myself to enjoy them and I'm not concerned about gaining a pound or two. It will all even out. I'm happy, and living happily in my skin is something that I didn't experience when I was obsessed about everything that I put into my mouth. Judging by the miserable expressions on the faces of some, they would be far better served to eat the damn cake, drink the G & T, and carry on with a pleasurable life.

Part of the pleasurable life is experiencing intimacy. When you are older and beginning a new intimate relationship, it is an experience of vulnerability and anxiety. Life changes the body, whether it be from weight gain, the effects of gravity, pregnancy and birth, or surgeries. Following relationships in which self-confidence and comfort with the body take hits, often we are traumatized and it makes new beginnings fraught with worry and stress.

After divorce and the end of another long-term relationship, two years of a global pandemic, an extremely stressful career, and navigating the changes of menopause, a new relationship with promise and intimate encounters meant facing fears and body doubt head on. Having done the work, reading Sonya Renée Taylor's book, *The Body Is Not An Apology*, I found myself still being really apprehensive about intimacy and revealing my flawed, 50+ year old body to a new partner.

This man is incredible, and no stranger to feelings of difficulty with himself, and still I found it really emotional and challenging to let him discover me. As always, a good dose of humor, eyes squeezed tightly shut, and jumping in with both feet to take the plunge were my fallbacks. Heavier than I'd prefer, not exercising as much because of a knee injury, scars and stretch marks all on my mind, I let this sweet man see my body. Keeping my eyes squeezed tightly closed, I felt his soft breath on my skin as he kissed my scars. A tear trickled out of the corner of my eye as I realized that my body truly is not an apology. My body is this amazing collection of cells that all come together to form the physical structure of a woman, a mother, a lover.

His reassurance that the things I see as flaws are simply a part of my story is empowering. The narrative of my life is that of a physical, earthly being – a nurturer of babies, strong and whole. He knows who he is, and he has added to my list of incredible humans that have helped me to reframe for myself that which is often considered unacceptable in our culture: to see myself as beautiful and desirable.

The healing journey and acceptance of self – comfort in my own skin and undeniable presence in this earthly realm – are an awesome part of who I have become.

Do I have moments of incredible self-doubt? Of course I do. But carrying on regardless means that at some point during the day, I forget about my self-doubt because I am wholly enjoying myself. During the summer of the bikini, while at my sister's cottage, we took photos of ourselves hanging out on Priscilla, the giant pink flamingo floatie. The laughter, the flipping off the toy into the waters of Georgian Bay, the hanging on for dear life while Priscilla the fickle b*tch overturned, popping back to the surface sputtering and giggling, all while rocking a bikini made for a good time.

In an exercise in overcoming feelings of vulnerability and summoning courage, I sent photos to a potential romantic partner. It was really uncomfortable. My imperfections were showing, and my head tilted back in raucous laughter, being my silly, authentic self. I could see all of the things about myself that give my pause for self-criticism. But because it was the real, raw and imperfect me, the pictures were well received and the comment was made that I looked like I was really enjoying myself. And I was. Fully and completely! There was no comment made about being able to see the slight roll of my tummy as I gripped the floatie trying to stay on. There was simply teasing about choking Priscilla out with the death grip I had around her neck. It was a new and amazing experience to be accepted as I am and considered enough just as I am.

As I move through this ongoing journey, I am excited – excited to embrace and celebrate who I am. I am me – just me – with imperfections and moments of bliss, contrasted with moments of grim self-doubt. Those moments inspire me to look deeper within, and to be more outrageous on the exterior. I will wear color. I will enjoy my body and its feelings and sensations. I will enjoy the evident discomfort that my self-acceptance and body bliss causes others. I am worth it. My body is worth it. If I reach just one human being who is struggling to love herself (or himself!) and her body, then I have done my job as an empathetic human being. The ultimate way to conquer the dysfunctional thinking and obsession with diet culture and weight is to become an influencer – a *positive* influencer.

Once embarrassed to be seen entering or exiting a store known for larger sizes (Um, hello?! The width of my shoulders alone makes buying a fitted top difficult in smaller sizes!), I now proudly look in those shops just as much as in the stores that carry smaller sizes. I don't hide those bags when I make a purchase, because:

1. I look fan-fucking-tastic in what I bought.
2. Mind your own fucking business, nosy parker.
3. I give zero fucks what anyone thinks!

I will not be defined by what the tag inside my clothes says. I just simply refuse. I am more than a body. And my body is a smokeshow anyway! I'm going to be honest: it does help that there are men who have told me that I'm a total smokeshow. Those are the good ones. The mature men who know that a woman's worth and sex appeal goes beyond a Barbie-like figure. Those that can see the beauty in curves and the softness of a mature body, one that is aging with as much grace as can be mustered. **The size of my body does not determine my feminine beauty, nor the intellect of my mind.**

There is nothing more attractive than wearing well-fitted clothes, tailored to your body, no matter what its size. Well-fitted clothes can make the difference between a day that makes me feel good as opposed to how I feel when wearing something too tight, or pulling in the wrong spot. I feel I need to add that wearing appropriate *ahem* undergarments makes a huge difference as well! Shopping in the stores that carry clothes that suit your personal style, in your size, and at the price point with which you are comfortable or can afford – is priceless.

Social media is starting to embrace diversity. There's a long way to go, but wasting time watching TikTok and all of the love of diverse bodies by both men and women demonstrates how the collective consciousness is beginning to change. I write from the point of view of a white, middle class woman who has long struggled to be thinner. But equally important is to recognize that there are many in smaller bodies, even seriously underweight bodies, that struggle with body image as well.

Diversity in our cultural consciousness is the goal, not just acceptance of heavier bodies. Recognizing the beauty of the body regardless of size, ability, colour, or gender is what is important! I encourage all women (and men!) to do a social media cleanse; unfollow any account that makes you feel like crap about your body just the way it is. Follow influencers who embrace diversity and acceptance. There are many accounts that share fashion, health, beauty, lifestyle, etc. that don't exemplify or glorify only tiny bodies and youth. Follow those! I promise that made a huge difference for me.

One of the ways that I have worked to accept my body as it is is through my yoga. Practicing yoga for a number of years before doing yoga teacher training was the piece that brought me peace for a long time. With the growing popularity of yoga, however, came the North American cultural ideal that all yogis are skinny white girls, with six pack abs, who could put their feet behind their head. The dichotomy of what yoga truly is, with what it has become in our western society, in some ways became a hindrance in my journey as well as a catalyst for self-acceptance.

I will never forget the feeling of shame as a yoga teacher poked my belly in a challenging new pose and sharply told me to suck in my stomach. I cannot move beyond the hot, face prickling feeling as I knew I was blushing in embarrassment, silently wishing the floor would open and swallow me. So before every class I teach, I vow to do better. To be accepting, to be open to the diverse bodies and abilities in every group. To offer simple modifications first, and only offering deeper expressions of each pose once the class has mastered the more gentle versions. To let my students know that wherever they are on that particular day, that is enough. They are enough and simply gorgeous as they are. I am open and I embrace my own perceived flaws, telling students when I am uncomfortable in a pose, or that my body doesn't like a version of something.

There are those in the wider yoga world who are making body acceptance and living in a larger body acceptable – even celebrated – for yogis. I applaud them and their undeniable vulnerability as they put themselves out there to be admired, followed, and also trolled and criticized. Those unkind comments hit a nerve; I don't care who you are. My mantra is be kind – to self, to others, and to our collective world.

As a well-educated, successful career woman, I am embarrassed that I have allowed obsession with my body to rule my life for so long. I know better. I know that what's important is on the inside. The outside is simply a vessel, a container that houses the heart, the soul, the intellect, feelings, and layers of self. What we see on the outside is but one facet of a human being. Attractiveness to others is perhaps at first because of our outward shell, but it should not be what fully defines us. Having the self-confidence to know that my outside is gorgeous and my inside is equally as beautiful is the equation that I choose to live by, and to define myself by.

I encourage others to embrace the body, no matter the size. Love the body you are in. It's the only one you have, and it serves you well. We are flawed, but our bodies deserve love and acceptance. If we don't love or accept ourselves, we open ourselves to the criticism and opinions of others. Carry yourself with confidence. Ignore the haters. Even better, give them the finger and carry on! That finger might be in your mind, or it could be your literal finger. I've been known to do both! Whatever you do, love yourself. It's hard sometimes, and you will falter, but it is truly the path to happiness.

Seriously, eat the carbs, drink the wine, wear the bikini and exclaim FUCK IT!!! Take your power back!

RELEASING THE WEIGHT
OF THE EXPECTATIONS
OF OTHERS IS THE ABSOLUTE
BEST WEIGHT TO *lose!*

# Chapter 13

## NIOMI MENDLER

Author Photo: Gary Paakkonen Photography
IG: @niomiroseanne

Hi, my name is Niomi. I am a single mama of two incredible tiny humans. Yeah, that's right, I created living breathing sassholes with my body. I am a fun-loving, smart ass, sarcastic, lover of wine, coffee, and buffalo plaid. I never take life or myself too seriously. I truly try to make the best of every situation. Life is far too short to care about what others think of you. In 2020, I dealt with postpartum depression, and I was also blindsided by my ex-husband asking for a divorce and leaving very quickly. The way I saw it, I had two options: sit in my self-pity and soak in the depression, or get up every day, chug some coffee, kick some ass, and heal myself. I chose the latter. Here I am today stronger than ever, loving myself again, and kicking some (metaphorical) ass!

I live for my babies. There isn't a decision that I make in my life in which I don't think about them first and how it affects them. I freaking live to see them smile! I knew from a very young age that I wanted to be a mother, so here I am kicking ass at momming, too. Just kidding. Momming is hard as fuck. As a divorced, single mother of two, I have had my fair share of struggles. I know I am not special, nor am I the first to experience my struggle. One thing that I am trying to learn to let go of, however, is downplaying or pretending like no one cares about my story. I have recently come to believe that everybody has a lesson, advice, or a story that someone else can benefit from. So here I am, writing this. My hope is to help inspire or uplift even just one person enough for them to start loving themself exactly how they deserve.

I like to believe that I have always been a very outgoing, happy, and, for the most part, confident woman. Well, when I sat down to write this, I stared at my MacBook screen for what felt like an eternity, just watching that blinking cursor…blink, blink, blink. It was taunting me, for sure. I had no idea where to start, but I just knew that I had so much that I wanted to say.

Not knowing how to start, I came up with a fun idea which I had a feeling might help me to build enough confidence to at least write a few sentences. I reached out to twenty of my closest female family members and girlfriends and asked them to simply give me three words that they felt best described me – no explanation needed, no further conversation about it after, just simply 3 words. Now, let me tell you, was it ever a boost of confidence and a truly self-building, humbling, and eye-opening moment for myself. When I started this chapter, I was at such a low and depressed point in my life that you can imagine how emotional it was for me to hear all these beautiful words from people. It was the exact motivation and fuel that I needed to get started.

The words that were repeated over and over by these women really helped heal me and motivate me to find the woman that I knew was still inside of me, under all the sad and broken layers – that woman that they all so deeply admired and loved. Some of the words that were repeated by most of them were words like: Passionate. Resilient. Strong. Loving. Funny. Fierce. Selfless. I saved all of these words as a list on my phone. I look back at it often when I am feeling lost or down about myself, as a simple reminder of who I am.

For whatever reason, it has become so taboo or frowned upon to speak positively about yourself. To hype yourself up. To empower yourself. People say that you are self-centered, full of yourself, or a narcissist. After doing this exercise and asking my lady tribe to describe me, I realized that if all of these women all see the same qualities and traits in me – qualities that they love and admire me for – why the freaking heck can't I think these things or see these things in myself, too?

I remember that day being such a huge pivot and shifting point in my healing and my journey to loving and finding myself again. I remember literally saying out loud, on my back deck, covered up under my buffalo plaid blanket, with a glass of red wine in hand, a candle beside me and my MacBook on my lap, "I need to be my own hype girl. Fuck anyone else."

I mean, don't get me wrong here. I have always had my seasons in my life where I was struggling or doubting myself, but for the most part I was raised by a team of supportive, encouraging parents. I say "team" because my mom and dad separated before my first birthday. They both remarried early in my life and are still happily married to those partners. In my eyes, I have always had four parents. They all haven't always seen eye to eye, but let me tell you, they all fiercely love and support the hell out of me! They do it every single day. They are the real MVPs in my life, for sure.

I've also always had a great group of friends – a group that always picks me up when I am down and reminds me who I am. But, regrettably and unfortunately, there was a long season that I allowed one person in my life to dull my sparkle and snuff out my fire. I allowed them to steal my confidence, make me question so much about myself, and lose who I truly am.

Since having my two beautiful children and going through my separation, every day has been a little bit of healing and learning to love myself again; all of me – every pound, every stretch mark, every piece of the broken heart, and every fallen tear – all over again. I mean, come on. It became clear that I needed to focus seriously on loving *myself* first.

I will never forget the day I found out that I was pregnant with my son – my firstborn, the boy who made me a mama. It was Mother's Day 2017. I was home alone; my children's father was out for the evening. I remember so clearly just feeling "different," with no other way to explain it. I believe it was my first experience of mother's instinct. I felt like my mind and body were trying to tell me something.

So, like most would, I settled in for a hot bubble bath and a casual pregnancy test. I ran my usual scalding hot bath, added the piles and piles of bubbles and Epsom salts, casually peed on a stick, set it on the edge of the bathtub (upside down, of course), got in, and waited. I remember flipping that test over and that feeling and the emotions when I saw the positive test is unlike anything I've ever experienced in my life. It's a moment nothing could ever come close to. I experienced that moment alone. I started my journey as a mother alone – sitting in my bathtub alone – and now, I thrive alone in my place as a single mother. I'm a strong as fuck mother of two. Although, if I am being brutally honest here – which is why I am pretty sure you're all here now – becoming a mother also started a four-year-long internal battle of me struggling to love myself again, and to love my body.

There will never be a time in my life that will ever come close to the feelings that I felt on the days that I had my two children. They are my "why." My strength, my heartbeat, my sun, and my bug, my everything. My oldest, my son, my sonshine, William. My little ladybug, my daughter, Charlotte. I had both of them via C-section. My first was an emergency section after 13 hours of unsuccessful labor. The second was a mandatory scheduled section due to unforeseen complications with my first C-section.

Unfortunately, the day that I had my son was a huge turning point in losing the love and respect that I should have shown my body. Now, hear me out here. Yes, the day I became a mother was the happiest day of my life, and undoubtedly one of the highest feelings I have ever experienced. I also look back and remember how disappointed and broken I felt that my body had let me down. My body couldn't do what I was *literally* made to do as a woman: have a vaginal birth. I remember so clearly, as I was coming in and out of consciousness while being wheeled into the operating room after a failed labor gone downhill, thinking to myself and worrying what others will think when I say that I had to have a C-section. I was so disappointed in my body for not holding up its end of the deal.

Thankfully, I fared well after the operation, but sadly my sweet tiny son wound up with a bed in the NICU. Now, after a C-section, you are in hospital for 48-72 hours regardless, so at least I was down the hall from him. It was a very long, painful hall to venture up and down dozens of times a day to nurse, change, hug, and love my tiny human when he should really, truly be in my arms and on me. Every time I got out of that bed and painfully walked to the NICU to see my sonshine, I remember holding back tears because I was so mad at my body, as this was not how I pictured the first few days of his life – and our lives together. Every time I saw him in that bed with the wires and monitors all over him, I blamed myself and my body.

Being a first-time mother in my blissful, new, and happy role, once I got home, I buried these feelings of disappointment and sadness deep down, and for the most part, I think it is safe to say, I forgot about them… but, oh boy did they ever catch up with me down the road.

I always seemed to have been comfortable with my body. I mean, not always confident, but comfortable nonetheless. I had my times where I'd wish I fit in something differently, something hugged my hips tighter, something lifted my boobies higher, or I looked sexier in an outfit. But don't we all do that? Here's a huge middle finger to the media for sexualizing women and our bodies so much.

During a time like pregnancy when I should feel beautiful and glowing and supported, I felt self-conscious; I felt ugly; I felt huge. I always felt like everyone was always staring at me and judging me. I felt unsupported, unappreciated, and unattractive at home. Plus, everywhere I went people would comment about "Wow, you're huge," "Sure that isn't twins?" "Looks like you're due any day now" and the words always dug in and hurt so deep, even knowing that no one meant it maliciously. It was me against my head, never being able to turn off the comments and negativity.

I spent so many hours staring at my naked body in the mirror, looking for stretch marks, covering my entire body in every stretch mark cream money could buy or comparing last week's photo to the next week's. I took weekly photos with both of my babies beginning from week 10 all the way to my first week postpartum. Every weekly photo was of me wearing the exact same dress...which led me to compare, day after day, week after week, month after month, and of course, the biggest evil: pregnancy to pregnancy.

No matter how often I looked in the mirror and tried to remind myself to be kind and give myself grace as I literally made human beings with my body, I still struggled to take my own advice. I mean, I made real-life, crying, eating, pooping, thinking, nose picking, snack demanding, temper throwing, belly giggling, and sass-filled human beings. I could never seem to allow myself the grace and love that I very well knew that I needed and deserved. Looking back, I feel that not fully being able to love and accept myself and my body for how beautiful and perfect it truly was had a lot to do with the environment I lived in and called home.

As corny and cliche as it may sound, I really feel like the saying, "Before you can love anyone else you must love yourself" truly applies so much to my life. There was so much time and years wasted looking for validation, love, and respect from places I never received it from. I recently went through a very emotional and intense time in my life.

2020 brought a whirlwind of emotions, experiences, and mess for everyone. For me it brought postpartum depression, an unexpected, blindsiding divorce, and my world being completely flipped upside down, chewed up, and spit out.

Part of that hard season for me was battling postpartum depression after the birth of my daughter in March 2020. I know the pandemic has taken a great toll on all of us. My experience is no different. My daughter's birth, as I said, was a mandatory scheduled C-section, so there was no avoiding the hospital. She was born a week after lockdown. Hospitals scared the crap out of me at that time because of the pandemic. My son at home, who has an underlying heart condition, was then considered high risk. The idea of being in the hospital with potential COVID-19 patients around any corner sent my anxiety into overdrive.

I will admit that the quiet, no-visitors alone time with just me, my brand new baby girl, and her father was blissful and much more relaxing than my experience with my son's birth. Unfortunately, that feeling very quickly wore off when I realized that I couldn't have any of my parents come meet and hold my daughter once I got home. As a matter of fact, no one could tell me how long it would be until anyone was able to come hold my daughter. My mom couldn't stay with me and help allow me to rest and recover from my birth. My friends couldn't come hold and snuggle the tiny human that I created. My family members could not come sniff the newborn baby goodness that I made.

We had countless visitors come to the door, driveway, stare through a window, or sit in the backyard. We had a sea of gifts, food, and coffee delivered. I had friends call daily to Facetime and check in on me. But every single time anyone left, without fail, as soon as that door would close, I would fall to the floor and cry my eyes out. I am tearing up now just remembering the pain that I felt inside and out. I had never felt so alone, trapped, and isolated. A newborn, a toddler, a C-section, struggling with my new body post-birth, a pandemic, raging postpartum hormones… talk about a recipe for disaster.

Looking back, I never reached out. I never asked for help. I internalized everything because I felt guilty, as everyone was experiencing depression or troubles due to the pandemic. So why were my issues any different? I battled postpartum depression silently and alone. I cried daily for hours. I would sit in my daughter's bedroom while nursing her and just cry while holding her. I felt so angry at myself. I should have been enjoying these days with her, but instead I was so depressed and so angry.

I had no help from my then-husband, who repeatedly told me that I needed to get over it or that I needed to stop crying, or that I needed to stop being angry, that there was nothing I could do about it and I was overreacting. I shut down with him and suppressed all those feelings from the number one person I should have been able to turn to. In retrospect, this all should have been a red flag for me for the pending divorce that he was silently planning.

It sounds so ugly for me to say this now, but when my ex-husband left us, the first thing I did was curse my body. I literally blamed the shape of my body and my physical appearance for my marital breakdown. How truly wrong I was. There were so many deep-rooted issues in our marriage that I didn't even see until after he left.

With that said, now we are both much happier. We have moved forward, and are in love with our new lives and our co-parenting. As you can imagine, it was quite a road to heal and accept it all.

After I gave myself grace and time to heal, I found myself. I found a woman inside who I didn't even know existed. Instead of depression and sadness, I chose me. I chose my babies. I believe that allowed me the opportunity to sit back and truly evaluate my life and what I was doing with it. Words that I never thought I would say, but find myself saying often: I am so grateful for my divorce and separation. It has been, by far, one of the greatest things that has ever happened to me. The first thing that I did was put my body, mind, and healing above everything else.

I'm a single mother of two. Although I truly believe that my babies come above all others and that their happiness truly equates to a lot of fulfillments in life, I also strongly believe that if I am not at my best, I can't show up for my children, which in turn that means that I can't give them what they deserve. There is not enough support out there to allow mothers, especially new moms, time to put themselves first. It's such a stigma.

For the first time since becoming a mother, I allowed myself to be selfish. I put myself first. My health. Both physical and mental. I focused on my own healing and whatever that looked like day to day for me. I knew that no matter what I needed, there was someone to help me with kids so that I could go for an 8km run, or take an hour bath, or go to a therapy session in the park on the phone (because COVID) while my parents watched the kids.

I put myself above everyone – including my own children – while I focused on myself and my own healing. I had the world's most incredible support system helping me day in and day out so that I could help myself heal and become a stronger, brighter, healthier, and more driven woman than I have ever been in my life.

The first step that I took toward finding my happiness and my whole self again was to rise above the depression and workout every single day. I mean, I really went for it. I woke up at 5am daily. I did not allow myself excuses. Some days I would work out in the middle of my living room with my son and infant daughter beside me, cheering me on and my son usually "participating." I mean, that toddler can really crush a burpee! I pushed through the hard days and on the good days I made sure to push myself a little bit harder. Putting my physical and mental health first truly helped me find such a deep part of myself that I forgot existed.

I started a program that was recommended to me by a friend. It was a boxing program, and I thought, *No way; there's no way that I can box.* I couldn't stop laughing when she suggested it. Then the next day I woke up and thought to myself, *Why the hell not? Let's do it.*

So, every day for six weeks I woke up and no matter how silly I felt punching fists in the air and high-kicking in the middle of my living room, I did it anyway. Each day passed and I got stronger, braver, and so much more confident. I started noticing that it wasn't even just the weight I was losing. I started noticing that the way I looked at my body was changing. The way I spoke to myself was improving, and I was feeling super badass.

I focused a lot on my nutrition, portion control, and being mindful of what I was fueling my body with. Don't get me wrong here, I have forever allowed myself all of the chocolate and wine. I never restrict my diet. I don't believe in "diets" or "dieting." I believe in being aware and making conscious choices to help your body feel its best. No human being is like the other, so we all respond differently to different workouts, food plans, and self-care. So, my advice is to just experiment and find what works for you, and holy hell, lady, give yourself grace and be patient.

I know so deeply that my children saved me. During the darkest, hardest, and lowest days of my life, my children kept me waking up, they kept me pushing, and they kept me surviving. One day that really hit me hard and clicked. *If it wasn't for my body, I wouldn't have these beautiful, fun, loving, silly, adventurous, exhausting, tiny humans.* Which, I am sure, seems like the simplest "duh" moment to some of you. But for me – the woman who stared daily at her pregnant and postpartum body in disgust and disrespect – this was a huge turning point in my life and my journey. It was the moment that I truly realized how grateful I am for my body and began loving myself in a way that I never had before.

I found a quote during my struggle that really stuck with me. I am unsure of the origin, but I hope it gives you the strength that it gave me:

"You've never seen this version of you. So, give yourself a little grace and breathe through it."

I can now truly say that I love myself. I care for myself in ways that I would not have before. I have evaluated so much of my life. I have surrounded myself with a group of loving, positive, and supportive people. I have found myself – the strong, passionate, fierce, resilient, loving, funny woman my friends and family all knew was inside me and gave me the little push and reminder about. I have found a good man who shows me true love in the deepest rooted meaning. He shows up and loves me and my babies in ways that I could have never even dreamed of.

When I look at myself in the mirror, when I try on my clothes, when I lift both of my beautiful babies up into my arms, when I see my tummy roll when I sit down, when I see my scar from my two C-sections that brought me my babies, I smile. I truly smile. I am so proud of this beautiful body I call my own. It has endured some intense shit; it's also been through some amazing shit, and every single day my body gets up and cheers me on – and damn, am I ever grateful for that.

With the beautiful love I have found, the bright new life I am building, and the amazing support system and positive outlook I have found deep in me that I didn't know existed, I know that I can keep kicking ass at loving myself and my beautiful body, one day at a time.

I am aware that every day is a new challenge on my journey to continuing to love myself and my body, but I am excited to face the good days and I know that I am strong enough to conquer the tough days. In the meantime, I will just be over here kicking ass!

THE SIZE OF MY BODY
DOES NOT DETERMINE MY
FEMININE BEAUTY, NOR THE
INTELLECT OF MY *mind.*

# *Chapter 14*

# SARAH CONNORS

Author Photo: Nicola Toon, Hulahoop Photography
sarahconnorsnd.com | IG: @drsarahconnorsnd

## THIS IS NOT YOUR ARMOR

Growing up I was a very shy, quiet, and introverted kid. I wanted nothing more than to be the proverbial wallflower, blending into the background where no one would see me. Not being seen seemed like the safest place for me at the time. I was also bullied from a very young age, and my bullies were boys. Both of them started out as my friends, but then something caused that to change into teasing, and then full on verbal and physical abuse over time. To give you an idea of the extent of it, my dad was concerned enough that he felt it was a good idea for my siblings and I to take karate lessons for a while so we had basic self-defense skills.

The lesson I took from that bullying was that I needed to be as invisible as possible and then maybe I would be safe. I know what you're thinking: why didn't I talk to a teacher or my parents? Well, I did, and the outcome of that was the bullying became worse. Again, the lesson I took from that was I needed to keep these things to myself, and hope I could make myself as invisible as I possibly could. Even at home I didn't feel completely safe. My sister and I didn't really get along growing up and she would tease me and push my buttons a lot. When I tried to mention it to my parents, I was told I was too sensitive and to grow a thicker skin. I didn't learn this until I was older, but I'm an empath and that means I feel very deeply - both my own emotions, as well as picking up on the emotions of others around me. This has served me well in my chosen career as a Naturopathic Doctor and Birth Doula, but as a kid growing up it often felt like hell on earth.

My name is Sarah Connors (yes that is my actual real name and yes I have heard almost all the Terminator jokes). As mentioned I am a Naturopathic Doctor and Birth Doula in my professional life. I am running my own practice, Seratauga Family Naturopathic, in collaboration with a few great multidisciplinary clinics that also share my values of providing quality healthcare to our patients. I am a sister, daughter, and Auntie in a pretty supportive family, and am fortunate to call most of my friends my "chosen additions to my family." I am also someone of mixed heritage, as I am Mohawk, Irish, Ukrainian, and quite likely a few other Western European lineages according to my grandmother, which has definitely influenced my life in big ways. The naming of my practice really highlights this influence. Not only was this a family effort, but Seratauga is actually a blend of the Mohawk and English spelling of the word, which roughly translates to "Healing waters of the Great Spirit." The reason I mention all of this is so you know a little bit more of who I am now, and that the rest of the story I am going to share with you is the journey of how I got here.

Heading back to where I was as a kid, unfortunately, I didn't know I was an empath, and how to deal with my emotions in a healthy way. As a result I ended up finding two main coping strategies to try and buffer things: eating my feelings (hello emotional eating for the next two decades) and running away from conflict. My family could see I was continuing to grow, putting on more weight than height, and they began to mention it to me. I know now this was coming from a place of love and concern, but what it fueled was a sense of shame and unworthiness that was growing even faster than my weight inside me. My desire not to be seen created what I call my "closet emotional eating patterns," where I would hide food that I ate outside of meals with my family. A common occurrence would be for me to eat an entire tub of Ben & Jerry's ice cream in an evening while watching TV by myself, and then burying the evidence in the garbage so my family couldn't see it.

There weren't many places I considered to be completely safe, but the music room in my high school was my literal sanctuary. I would spend my lunch hours and pretty much any time I wasn't in class in the music room because my bullies didn't go to the music room. I don't think I would have many happy memories of high school if it wasn't for that room and the wonderful teachers who ran our music program. Mr. and Mrs. Goodwin, thank you for helping to provide a lifeline for kids like me that really needed a safe space. I also loved music, and being a part of the high school band became a big part of my life when I was in high school. Most of my friends were in band or the music program. However, as much as I wanted to, I couldn't stay in my sanctuary forever. Eventually I had to make my way out into the halls, and again deal with my tormentors.

I wasn't consciously aware of this at the time, but what I've come to realize over time is that part of me thought if I could "build armor" - aka the extra weight I started to gradually put on my body starting at 11 years old - then maybe I would be safe. Maybe the boys would leave me alone because I wouldn't be desirable. Maybe I could blend into the background because I wasn't anything special to look at. Again, this wasn't anything I was consciously aware of at the time, but it's something I have come to have awareness of as I've gotten older - when I finally decided to stop running away from myself. The messages I internalized from being bullied were that I wasn't good enough, I wasn't worthy of positive attention, and I wasn't worthy of love.

Since my bullies were boys this made things even more challenging going through puberty. I was simultaneously attracted to boys and afraid of them. If you weren't a male member of my family, or some of the few males I managed to build a positive relationship with, I didn't trust you. This theme played out on loop in wanting to have a romantic relationship but also being too afraid to really try.

I was in undergrad by the time I actually tried to have a relationship. Even though I was living in one of the best places to meet really great people, I was still terrified of putting myself out there and risking being hurt. By this time, my "armor" had grown to a considerable amount and was still growing.

University was a great time in my life. I had such an amazing opportunity to grow as a person and build some of the best friendships that I still have and treasure to this day (with both men and women). Unfortunately, I still had my armor and I continued to add to it over that time. Even though I was no longer being bullied, the internalized messaging from my youth was still very much there. As a result of my self-loathing and poor coping skills, I was well on my way to 230 lbs by the end of my undergraduate studies (and would eventually hit almost 270 lbs at my heaviest).

No self-sabotage is complete without also adding in the wonderful stories of diet culture on top of all of this. I was aware I was heavier than I should be, and I didn't like my body at all. In addition to continuing to eat my feelings and hide my food from people, I of course went through progressive regimens of diet and exercise to try and curb my bulge. Through all of this I was becoming a yo-yo dieter like so many women in North America. I also became extremely discouraged by my lack of success and eventually became convinced that I just didn't have what it takes to reach a healthy weight. This didn't stop me from relapsing both ways - going through periods of ra-ra motivation where I thought *this time will be different,* and *this time I can do it* - only to be met by a later loss of motivation and further disappointment with myself as the "evidence" piled up that I was clearly a failure when it came to weight loss.

Enter the end of 2019/beginning of 2020. That's right, the achilles heel of almost every person who wants to lose weight...the New Year's Resolution. Obviously I had set and reset this New Year's Resolution a multitude of times like just about every other person out there. Then something happened in February 2020 that triggered the dominos to finally fall in a different direction. I didn't find the "holy grail diet plan" - it actually started with one of the worst events that can happen to a person: a pretty bad car accident.

Driving to a morning networking meeting, I hit black ice and spun my car out in the most fantastic way. By some miracle I managed to spin my car across 3 lanes of traffic, hit a cement median, and spin back across those same 3 lanes of traffic and hit the other cement median without hitting any other cars or seriously injuring myself. I was in such a state of shock, it took most of my family and several other people to convince me to go and get checked out at the hospital. As I mentioned, by some miracle I had no major injuries. I was slightly bumped and bruised and shocked, but otherwise fine. My car, on the other hand, was not - it was a complete write off.

At this point I was feeling pretty low. I needed a vehicle to get around for work, and my financial picture did not look promising for finding a good replacement vehicle that I could afford. I have always been someone who believes in hope, that somehow things will work out. I know this sounds strange coming from someone who grew up with bullying. I guess despite that I still learned from all the other experiences in my life that, generally, things work out. In this situation, though, I have to admit that my positive outlook was more glass half empty than half full. Fortunately, the Universe, the powers that be, whatever you prefer to call it, had everything planned out. I just didn't know it yet.

Just before the accident happened, I had been looking at a self-development program run by a thought leader I had come across online. I had heard Jim speak as a guest on another podcast I listened to, and then started listening to his podcast when it launched. I had wanted to join his program (the Transformational Coaching Program, or TCP) for a while already, but I couldn't bring myself to invest the money in TCP when I didn't have it. However, because I was interested I kept myself on the mailing list and figured I would do the program one day. As I was figuring out all the paperwork for the insurance claim, the emails started coming into my inbox that TCP would be open for enrollment again. At first, I didn't pay any attention to it because my priority at that time needed to be figuring out how to replace my car with whatever money I received for the car I lost. I figured I would just follow the free training, and then next time the program came available I would enroll then if I could. However, something was nagging at me that I needed to do this. I needed to enroll.

Now remember, this made no logical sense. I still needed to replace my car and the investment in the course was most of what I had received from the insurance payout for the car. This was when the Universe really started to conspire with me. As I was looking for a car I posted on Facebook that I was looking for a vehicle and if anyone knew of a vehicle for sale at a good price in good condition, to let me know. One of my friends saw the post and reached out to me to let me know that they had recently bought a new vehicle and were looking to sell their old vehicle. I was so excited and grateful.

This worked out so well, I actually had some money left over after I bought the vehicle. It was not enough to pay for the program in full, but just as I was figuring out what to do with the small amount left over, the email came in. There would be a payment plan option for the program I wanted to join and the enrollment period was closing soon. Now, obviously, the logical thing to do would have been to do something else with that money, but something told me I just had to use some of it to enroll.

Despite all the fear, I trusted my intuition and I joined the program. I was feeling slightly ill but mostly excited for the rest of the week. I managed to do BOTH: find a great car and join the program that I knew would be a game changer for me. I was feeling pretty good about life at this point, all things considered. Then enter the first lockdown of the COVID-19 pandemic. The world essentially shut down, and I had no idea how I was going to make all of this work. Again, the logical thing to do would be to figure out if I could get my money back, defer the program, or whatever I needed to do, but again something told me it would all work itself out. I trusted my intuition and kept going, and thank the Creator/Universe I did! This amazing program ended up absolutely changing my life in just about every way, including my relationship with my weight and my body.

Several weeks into the program on a group call I ended up getting one of the individual coaching spots they would offer during the group calls. I had been learning lots, and starting to feel myself shifting and changing, but this call would start one of the biggest changes I would experience in TCP, and in my life so far. As I started talking to the coach on the call, she asked me, "Why do you think you are still hiding? What's keeping you from showing up?" At the beginning of TCP we were told to focus on one of two areas: business or health. Being in the middle of a pandemic and most of the world being shut down, including my practice, I figured business was more important than worrying about my weight. I was talking about being nervous to show up online, do live content, or anything where I would be seen in a more visible way. Remember, I spent the majority of my growing up years trying to blend into the background.

The idea of putting myself out there more was hella scary. As I'm thinking about her questions, my first thought is *I don't know, that's why I am here,* but one of the earlier lessons in the program was that "I don't know" doesn't actually help you so I can't answer with that. I come out with, "I'm afraid of what other people will say. I'm afraid of judgment," thinking back to being bullied. I then mention growing up with that and how that affected me. She nodded, and then she said, "Do you think it could be something else? Would you describe yourself as someone who loves themself?" This question hit me like a ton of bricks. Love myself? Love myself? At first I was quietly thinking, then from what seemed like out of nowhere to me at the time, I started to cry. *Why am I crying? Why am I crying in front of all these people? Everyone is staring at me, they must think I'm crazy.* My internal dialogue was going absolutely nuts. The coach was just sitting there, waiting for me to speak. *I have to say something, she's waiting for me to say something.* Come on, Sarah, people are waiting!

I wiped away my tears furiously, and breathed to calm myself. The chat box on the side was filled with caring, compassionate comments, supporting me as I felt some of the most vulnerable feelings I had ever felt in front of hundreds of people online.

I finally answer, "I, I don't think I do love myself." I couldn't speak anymore, the tears and emotions were welling up in my throat, and I was fighting to keep it all at bay. The coach smiled kindly and said, "Well, then, that's where you need to start." One of the resources shared with us in TCP is a list of recommended books. After my declaration of lacking self-love, I was reminded by the coach and the collective of the book in the list called "Love Yourself Like Your Life Depends On It" by Kamal Ravikant. Once I got off the coaching call, I decided to download the audiobook and start listening to it right away. I was still feeling very raw emotionally from the call, and thought maybe a walk while listening to the audiobook would help. I ended up listening to the entire book that afternoon/evening and I cried more than I had cried in a very long time.

The floodgates had finally opened, and the pain I had been eating and carrying for all those years was pouring out.

This became my turning point.

As I started to recognize that the actual root of my "problem with weight" - the root of my physical body armor that I had built pound by pound to protect my sensitive heart from the world - was actually stemming from a lack of self-love, my relationship with my body completely changed. All the struggle to "lose the weight" I so desperately wanted to lose melted away. Over the remainder of the program and the months that followed, I dug into the tough work of developing self-love and releasing self-hate. As I did, the armor I had been carrying for so long slowly started to fall away. I had always scoffed at people that said losing weight was easy when you figured out what worked for you, because I had never figured out this secret. The task always felt impossible to release weight and not have it come back like a boomerang you don't want.

Little did I know my key to "losing the weight" and building a positive relationship with my body was loving myself. Just so you are aware, I put "lose" or "loss" in relation to weight in quotations because I know that's the language most people are familiar with seeing. In my personal and professional life I use it as little as possible now because the subconscious mind interprets the word "loss" as something that is "lost" and I need to go and find it again. This thereby programs us to remain yo-yo dieters by the language we use - hence why I use different language now, like "releasing" weight. Since learning these lessons, I work to embody them in everything I do - especially my relationship with my body. I used to dread working with patients on weight, but now I get excited about it. I even built my first ever online program around releasing weight the healthy way, rooted in uncovering the subconscious stories and beliefs we hold that are sabotaging our relationship with our body. Releasing the weight, aka my armor, has become "easy" for me because I now understand I actually care about myself and my body. They often say you can only teach something if you've first learned it yourself. Something I often ask my patients now is if they care about themselves and their bodies. I ask this because something I learned through my journey was that I didn't take care of myself - because, at my core, I didn't truly care about myself. Why would I bother taking care of something like my body that I didn't care about?

Now I am able to prioritize healthy eating and moving my body because behind it isn't self-loathing, but self-love. As I continue to cultivate that relationship with myself I am learning to actually truly love myself for me, as I am. Releasing the weight that no longer serves me has become a great side effect as opposed to the sole focus. We are all worthy of self-love, always, and the more we can lean into that and grow that relationship with ourselves, the more we can love our body - no matter the shape or size.

# Chapter 15

## VICKY JOMAA

Author Photo: Jamie Cornish
theselfcareshop.ca | IG: @vickyjomaa

Do you know what's funny? The very first time I had set aside to sit down and write about this journey of self-love and body acceptance happened to land in the middle of a freaking historical heatwave. As I sit here with a slightly blank mind wondering how to start, sitting in my thoughts, I find it ironic that I'm doing so in boxer shorts with my cellulite and thigh dimples in full force, in a sports bra with my belly rolled slightly over the waistband. Don't even get me started on the boob sweat. This is next-level.

I am a literal hot mess right now.

"Journey" seems like a good word for all of this because, let's be honest, accepting and appreciating our bodies is a lifelong journey. But here is the thing: it's not like we ever "get there." There is no final destination on this journey. Loving ourselves and the bodies we are in isn't a destination; it IS the journey.

We make a daily choice to accept and love our bodies, no matter where we are in life. I am not saying that we will always be happy with them, because we won't. I am not saying that we won't cry that something doesn't fit anymore, because we will. I am not saying that we won't catch that glimpse in the mirror and wish for something different, because we will. What I am saying is that we deserve to learn to love ourselves so fiercely that even when we are feeling those things, we can take that deep breath and whisper to ourselves so authentically and unapologetically, "I love you, no matter what."

We are forever evolving and changing, and that is a beautiful thing. I know that sometimes it's hard to really believe that, but stay with me. You are beautiful, and your body is honestly the least interesting part about you.

For me, this path to body bliss was really one about self-love. I realized that I needed to love myself so unapologetically and ferociously before anything else was possible. How can we accept ourselves, inside and out, without self-love? I need to love me – ALL OF ME – in order to feel truly happy and fulfilled. There is a freedom in this choice, a magical sense of whimsy that when we start to experience it, we want more of it.

Well, I quickly discovered that this involved loving my outside just as much as I loved the person inside. Body acceptance is self-love, and self-love involves accepting our bodies. I didn't just come up with this out of nowhere, by the way. It was shaped from experiences and lessons – and HARD WORK.

Our perspectives in this life are completely a choice (which is a life lesson in itself!), but we only gain the wisdom to start making different choices in our perspective by learning lessons – and those lessons come from experience.

I have experienced that self-love is self-care, and self-care is HARD. But one of the best things I have ever heard and truly taken to heart is that we can do hard things (can I get a fuck yes?!).

So now that I am older and wiser, I am able to choose my perspective on my own body, loving myself, and taking care of myself. That wasn't without the journey beforehand, though, including the choices I had to make, and the lessons I've learned from those experiences.

My name is Vicky, and as a woman, mother, wife, and life coach, my journey is not one that involves the size of my jeans, numbers on the scale, or an endless list of failed fad diets. In fact, I do not care at all what the numbers are on my clothes. I have a good relationship with food, and I work out regularly doing things I enjoy.

So you might be wondering what my journey involved if it wasn't about any of those things. I get that for many, those things are a part of their journey. For me, motherhood played a major role. I have certainly learned more from being a mom and those tiny humans that I brought into this world than anything else, so most of my profound and epiphany-like moments circled around motherhood in some way, shape, or form (not all, but most).

Narrowing this down into one chapter was hard, but there are a few lessons that I have taken away over the years when it comes to this topic of body bliss that I wish to share with you. This is just part of my story. I don't have it all figured out. I don't have it all together all of the time. None of us do. We likely never will. We are imperfectly perfect in our own unique paths, and I can only hope that as you read these stories from all of these incredible women, that you also realize that you deserve to love yourself to the fullest degree – inside and out.

## THE MAGIC OF NOT GIVING A F*CK ABOUT WHAT OTHER PEOPLE THINK

We don't have enough time on this earth to spend our lives giving a shit about other people's opinions. What we wear, how we look, and the perspective we have of our bodies and appearances have been dictated by media and external validation factors for FAR too long. UGH. Rant over. Just kidding; it's just starting.

Exhibit A. Shorts. I hate shorts. You know what I am talking about. They ride up too high; they show too much; we don't like how we look in them… blah, blah, blah. Experiences, as I said before, shape us.

So here's a little background information on how shorts played a role here. I am an extremely fair-skinned individual. I was born blue-eyed, blonde-haired, and with porcelain skin that you could almost see through. As I grew up and wore shorts or skirts that showed my legs, do you know what people commented on?

How pasty and pale my skin was. Yep, seriously. A young, growing girl that was just trying to be comfortable in the summer heat faced these comments ALL THE TIME. From anyone and everyone.

It started off as feelings of embarrassment. It only grew from there.

I started associating my fair skin with being ugly compared to tanned skin, or people with different skin tones. My friends weren't getting comments about how pale their skin was. I was taught that I was only pretty if I was tall, blonde (tick one thing off the list), with big boobs (we will get to this later) and tanned skin. Thanks, society!

I just wasn't what I felt our current society deemed pretty, so I covered it up. I know now as a more grown and mature woman how misguided this all was, but you know what? That was the knowledge, experience, and conditioning that I had at the time. Being told you're pale or pasty does not make you feel pretty or attractive, especially as a child and teenager. I know this time in our lives is crucial; we go through so much during these years and so much of it is based on vanity metrics. For me, it was my fair skin.

For others, it was their unruly, curly hair.

Or their freckled skin.

Or their skin color in general.

Or the size of their waist.

Or the way people told them they ate too much.

Or too little.

Or needed to lose weight.

Or gain it.

Society, please stop commenting on children's features. We will think about it literally for the rest of our lives, and it teaches us to focus on the WRONG THINGS.

Fast-forward to this unusually hot summer (we are now 2.5 decades deep in strategic skin covering to avoid comments about how I glowed in the sun), with my five-year-old son picking out which pair of shorts to wear, and I was, as per usual, picking out which pair of yoga pants would be the least hot. I was mumbling to myself about how warm and uncomfortable I was when he said...

*"Well why don't you just wear the shorts?"*

Well, fuck.

This little mini of mine had inherited my fair, porcelain skin, blonde hair, and blue eyes. He was a striking little boy version of me. It was at that moment that I realized this tiny human could be conditioned to think the very same thing about his complexion that I struggled with practically my entire life. What if all he focused on was covering up like me because all people commented on was his fair skin?

Motherhood has this strange way of slapping you in the face sometimes. These unexpected moments come in hard and fast, and suddenly a lifetime of shaping and conditioning from our physical attributes being commented on is facing you square in the eye.

I could never let his perspective be the one that I had for so long that made me small in my own thinking, in my own skin. So at that moment, I realized that I had an opportunity. Why am I putting the thoughts and opinions of others – mostly strangers, I might add – ahead of my own comfort and choices? I made a choice. I changed it.

I stopped giving a fuck what other people's opinions were about my body.

What if the girl with the unruly, curly hair rocked it, instead of spending her life trying to straighten it?

What if the girl with freckled skin showed it off, instead of being embarrassed about it and finding full coverage foundations to cover it up?

What if the girl who was told she ate too much listened to her body's signals about hunger instead of spending her life counting calories?

What if we didn't have to sit here thinking about what could have been different if we were taught to not comment on people's appearances?

What if we knew then what we know now about how these comments can change the trajectory of our self-image?

This experience with him that day gave me the lesson that we can change our narratives for not only ourselves but the upcoming generation. It also gave me an opportunity to change my perspective, which in turn made me love myself a little more that day.

I let it all go – all those years of thinking that I just looked pasty and pale, and even ugly, because of it. I might be fair, but I am healthy and beautiful, too.

I took a deep breath and said to myself, "I love you, no matter what."

So, we both wore the damn shorts.

I will now be more conscious of comments related to physical appearances. Not just for myself, but with how I will teach my children to approach how they speak to others, themselves, and how they can cope with comments made to them as well.

And I hope that now he can also grow up not giving a fuck about what other people think.

## MIRRORS & MOTHERHOOD

I told you that some of my greatest lessons involved motherhood in some way, shape, or form. There is no reality check or justice in this world quite like when you make a human that becomes a tiny version of yourself that you can see coming to life in a way you had never thought possible. The whole "I'm turning into my mother" thing is real. (I love you, Mom.)

As a mom to a little girl, I instantly began to fear for her, as we often do as parents. I feared for her self-image. I feared for the pressures that she would face from a society that dictated to her what it thought she should look like. I feared for her equality. Her rights. Her everything.

Motherhood is a catalyst for great reflection. We begin to see ourselves and our world in a different light – knowing that what we model is what these small humans will begin to believe as truth, which will mold their perspectives and opinions for, well, pretty much everything.

Wow, talk about responsibility.

The moment she was born, I began to reflect on all of these things – my perspectives, my opinions, my self-talk – and how these very things would begin to shape her existence.

Let me tell you, this is not an easy thing to work through during postpartum. At a time when our bodies have done so much for this life, it's hard to look past the soft protruding belly, the wider hips, and the weird skin things that creating life does to you. Oh, and the hair loss – as if my hair wasn't struggling enough from the years of bleach abuse I infringed on it thinking that platinum blonde was the only way for me to look "hot." HAHA. I cringe at all those pictures now.

Having a child is like having a mirror placed in front of your life. Postpartum is one hell of a rollercoaster that we never wanted to go on, but ultimately knew we would have to in return for motherhood.

That's when the idea of this life mirror went from being a metaphor, to a literal event. I remember one day when my girl was about three, I caught her looking in the mirror hanging on the wall. She was wearing her birthday suit as she had just gotten out of the bath, but she stayed there for a moment. Like, a long moment. I knew that look.

She was looking at her body.

My heart sank.

Could it really be happening this young? I started going through the memory Rolodex in my mind wondering if I had recently made comments about myself in front of her, said anything negative about my body, or talked about literally anything physically related to my body or anyone else's that could have triggered this sponge of a human to stand in front of the mirror like that. I couldn't think of anything, because let's face it, we say those things in such a passive manner that they often don't stick out, and frankly, my mind was already overflowing at this point so I really shouldn't try and pinpoint an exact trigger here. Sigh. Anyway...

It is amazing how many thoughts your brain can shuffle through in a split second. At this moment it was as if time had stopped so that I could have an entire conversation with myself on how to handle this. And so I started thinking, how often do we stand in the mirror, analyzing every bit of us? Head to toe, side to side? When I said mirror, I meant metaphorically, but it turned literal quite quickly. Mind-blowing, right? Here we were actually looking in the mirror, yet it was a total reflection on my own life and how I talk to myself. When we look in that mirror and start to notice how that outfit fits, or how our hair looks, what are you telling yourself? Is it positive? Are you giving yourself a mental compliment, or are you telling yourself that you wish you were ten pounds smaller? Perhaps that you wish your hair was straighter, or curlier, because whatever we do have, we always seem to want the opposite – or maybe you noticed a new wrinkle.

I couldn't fathom my daughter staring in that mirror thinking anything bad about herself at such a young age. I mean, she was only three, right? But here's the thing: it starts that young. Even though maybe we can't specifically remember these events when we judged ourselves as kids, we can almost, without doubt, say that we likely started judging our features and bodies at a very young, tender age. Judgment and vanity metrics were all around us. It was the commercials on TV, the pictures in all the magazines, stores, and billboards – it was always just there.

So I ran to her, bent down to her eye level, looked in the mirror with her, and took a deep breath.

"You are so beautiful," I said. "And I love you."

She toddled her buck-naked self off into the hallway and said, "Love you too, mama!" while I shed a few silent tears. In that split second, I chose OUR perspective of self-love because of the lesson I wanted her to walk away with. I wanted her to look in that mirror and believe she was beautiful. In return, I knew I had to make different choices for myself when I looked in the mirror. I deserved that. She deserved that. She deserved a mom who could look at herself with confidence and grace, to show her that she can, too. I cannot change the fact that she will also grow up, likely analyzing her every feature in the mirror, overthinking what people say, and obsessing over what other people look like in comparison to herself. But I can, at the very least, model a few things for her (and for myself) that show her that even when we do those things, we can turn it around and still choose to love our bodies, no matter where we are in life.

So I took a deep breath and said to myself in the mirror, "I love you, no matter what."

## I CAN CHANGE SOMETHING ABOUT MY BODY IF I WANT TO

I want everyone out there to know that IT'S STILL OKAY TO WANT TO CHANGE SOMETHING ABOUT YOUR BODY. I have to shout that from the rooftops right off the bat. **Body bliss is not an either/or thing. It is okay to love your body AND still want to change something about it.** It is okay to accept your body the way it is and still have goals or wants based on your physical appearance. Loving ourselves and our bodies doesn't mean we can't do anything to it/for it/about it. Period. We can have both. I will have my damn cake and eat it too on this one.

Some things we can control, and others, we can't. Sometimes the things that we can control make us feel good. They can bring us that boost of confidence when we see ourselves in a picture or in the mirror. You know what I'm talking about – those days when you're like *DAMN my hair looks good.* Or *wow, this outfit makes my ass look GREAT.*

Or, when you're me, and you look at your boobs for the first time and say *WOW. They look normal.*

We are allowed to make choices for our bodies on the outside that could deeply help us heal on the inside. Owning this changed my life.

Okay, here it goes…

I knew my entire life growing up that something wasn't quite right when I looked in the mirror. (there's that darn mirror again, always showing me things). I am not even sure how to explain it. I wasn't oblivious; boobs were everywhere. Movies, magazines, TV… it wasn't hard as a young girl to notice what our bodies changing leads to. Idealistic women's bodies were seen everywhere we looked.

Mine didn't change the way it was supposed to. Parts of it did, but others didn't. I always thought that maybe they just weren't done developing yet and I was still stuck in that "awkward phase" when it came to a few things. And so began the years of being strategic when picking out shirts, finding ways to pad bathing suits so they looked normal, and figuring out how to turn my body in certain ways when I was fooling around with my boyfriend in an effort to never expose my front (sorry, Mom and Dad, I know you are going to read this).

But what I thought was the awkward phase or this "mid-phase" of development – apparently wasn't. It just *was*. Suddenly, I couldn't use puberty and the term "late bloomer" anymore. I was past that. I was grown.

These were apparently just my boobs.

I have one more quick public service announcement. This has NOTHING to do with the size of your breasts. Just no. I will get to that. Hang with me; this is hard to talk about.

Fast-forward to my early twenties. I am engaged – and boom! – pregnant (wow, that escalated quickly).

That lingering intuition was growing. Something still wasn't right. The girls just weren't doing the things that I kept hearing were supposed to happen when you get pregnant.

Aren't they supposed to get bigger?

Or tingle or something?

Or hurt?

What about my nipples? Does anything change with those bad boys?

The years that I had spent suppressing that inner voice were no longer and now it was screaming louder. I felt years of body image issues and emotions creeping to the surface, so I tried to say something to my doctor.

"Nothing is wrong. You're perfectly normal," they told me.

What am I supposed to say after that? I'm 22 and not a doctor.

I couldn't breastfeed. No, really... I couldn't. I did EVERYTHING right. No one believed me. Just give her a bottle. Try these cookies. Stop giving her a pacifier. See a lactation consultant.

So I did. I did ALL the fucking things!

I began hating this part of my body even more. I mean... HATE. I couldn't contain the dread that I felt over them. I hated how they looked, how they made me feel, and NOW, I couldn't even use them to feed my daughter. The ONE biological thing that they were intended for didn't even work and I had no idea why.

I was devastated.

Some things are out of our control, but that doesn't lessen the feelings and emotions that we have about our bodies. It actually makes them that much more infuriating.

Now, a lot of life happened for me over the next few years. I went to school, changed careers, got divorced, and remarried. Holy shit, right?! Us women, when we do something big, we do it REALLY BIG. The lessons and life experience from all of that will have to be in another book. We have a mission here *wink wink*.

We get wiser as we get older. We learn to embrace ourselves more than the opinions of others. This is one thing about aging that I can really get behind.

When I got pregnant with my second child, the two decades of previous body dysmorphia around this topic bubbled to the surface again. Only this time, thinking back to my experiences and lessons learned, and with a slightly wiser and clearer vision of life, I realized that I was the one and only person who could properly advocate for my health and need for answers.

Naturally, I turned to Doctor Google. Oh boy. You know you've done this too. Going down the Google search black hole is a kind of crazy we completely inflict on ourselves, but you know what? I needed something. I needed something that I could run with and go "HEY. I THINK THIS COULD BE IT."

One day, in the deepest, darkest corner of the internet, I found that *something*. It was a forum with a woman whose description of her experiences was practically identical to mine.

HOLY SHIT. This is it. I FOUND THE SOMETHING.

In comes Google search #2. I researched every doctor in my city that I could find that had any experience with women's bodies, breastfeeding, boobs, etc. When you get a breakthrough for something you have been searching for your entire life, you don't give up on it. I was on a mission.

I found a name (thank you, Google).

I took this name to my OB and demanded a referral. I didn't take no for an answer. This doctor usually only saw postpartum patients for very specific needs, but I didn't retreat until they said "Okay, we will get you in." I had to fight for it.

Beautiful friend reading this, you are your own best advocate. Trust your intuition. You know your body best. Fight for it.

Looking for rationale and answers can be a funny thing. As desperately as we want finite explanations, there is always a part of us that wants absolutely nothing to come of it.

If we get the answer, it means we were right (and then now what?) If we don't, it means we were wrong (no one likes to be wrong, and we still then want something to be the reason for why we felt this way our entire lives).

So the day finally came. I got to see the elusive boob doctor.

I will never forget that moment in my life. I was pregnant AF, sitting with this doctor. She looked at me, and within 5 seconds told me EXACTLY what I had.

Really? Like seriously? WTF.

I had spent 20 years battling this feeling, and in FIVE SECONDS, you had the answer?

You can change something about your body if you want to. It doesn't mean that you don't love yourself. It doesn't mean that you don't accept yourself. You can have both. We have autonomy over our bodies and the choices and perspectives we make for them. Period.

I have a form of breast hypoplasia that I was born with. There was nothing I could do about it. There is no way to know until post-puberty because that is when the physiological traits become apparent. It has NOTHING to do with size, at all. It affects physical attributes, as well as the mechanics of breasts, which explains why I couldn't breastfeed. I could have eaten 3 tonnes of milk cookies, drank gallons of milk production tea, and taken all the milk boosting medications that modern medicine has to offer; it wouldn't have made a difference. There was nowhere for those milk-making messages in my body to go to. They were at a dead end.

Suddenly, everything was explained.

I left that appointment as fast as I could and ugly cried in a way that I had never ugly cried before. I felt devastated, yet relieved to know the answer. I finally felt the years of mom guilt over formula feeding start to wash away, and a new wave of empowerment and acceptance came over me.

This is becoming more common than you think. The more I open up about it, the more women I discover with similar experiences who always felt like they had no one to talk to. They felt like they were alone, and that something was just wrong with them. Nothing is wrong with us. We do not need fixing. We need open minds. We need nothing to be taboo. We need love and acceptance from within, and information on what bodies are actually used for, not simply what they look like.

I can change something about the outside of my body that will deeply affect how I feel on the inside.

I had my sweet boy and gave him as much breast milk as I could with what little supply I had. I found as much donor milk as my limited time allowed and my dear husband drove around the city picking it up for me. One thing I do have to say is that I could produce colostrum like a boss. I had a freezer full of syringes of this liquid gold that I proudly expressed into the inside of his little cheek.

Until it was all gone, and I no longer had the time or energy to find sufficient amounts of donor milk. It was time to bring out the formula.

For years growing up, I had thought about getting a breast augmentation. Knowing now that this was about more than just bigger boobs and implants, I sought out a cosmetic surgeon in the city I lived in who was familiar with breast deformities. Yep, you read that right; the medical world classifies hypoplasia as a "deformity."

I would like to give the person who decided this a big middle finger. You suck.

I underwent breast augmentation and mastopexy to achieve the best results in creating a natural shape and size for my body type. My surgeon was wonderful, and I have never trusted this deepest, darkest part of my insecurity with anyone else before. When I told my husband that I wanted to do this surgery, all he said was "Okay, let me know what you need from me. I support you." I couldn't have asked for a better partner.

I had a friend who underwent a cosmetic breast augmentation that took me bra shopping for the first time at 31 years old. I felt that I could confide in this friend as she had gone through a similar surgery and it felt good talking to someone I could trust. I say "for the first time" because this was truly the first time I was buying a real bra, fitted to fit me. There was no gaping, no padding, and no need to be strategic. I just needed one that fit. And until now, I had no clue how to tell what fit and what didn't.

Sharing my story with her brought me back to my teenage years. I retreated a bit in age that day, just so I could let someone walk me through the experience as if I were a young girl again, experiencing something for the first time that I should have looked forward to, not dreaded. I chose to be grateful for that experience, and not grieve anymore that I didn't get it sooner.

Doing this surgery gave me something that nothing else could. I no longer think about the neckline of my shirts gaping when I bend over. I no longer dread finding a bathing suit that fits my entire body, not just certain parts, and then I have to alter the top. I no longer think about strategic positioning during sex (again, Mom and Dad, so sorry).

When it comes to your body, you know it best. No one else knows it as you do. Trust your intuition with it. Be your own best advocate. Fight for answers if you need them. Listen to yourself. Your voice matters more than anyone else's when it comes to your body and the choices you make for it.

You can change something about your body if you want to. Get your boobs done. Get the botox.

Lose the weight, gain the weight. New nose? No problem. It doesn't change who you are. Your body is the least interesting thing about you, and we are allowed to make choices for ourselves on the outside that can help us heal on the inside. I got this done for myself, and only myself, to allow me to experience a feminine side of me that I felt was missing for my entire life. It allowed me to shed the years of mom guilt, of wondering what was wrong, and letting go of the hurt and pressure that I had put on myself all of these years over what my body should look like.

I will forever remember the moment that I looked at myself for the first time after I took that surgical bra off. "Wow," I said. "They look normal." I took a deep breath and said, "I love them." (This time, I already knew that I loved myself.)

Ah, that body bliss. Those moments where we look at ourselves and own it. Own it ALLLLL. The rolls, the freckles, the soft spots, the hard parts, the big parts, the small parts. Our bodies might sometimes give us physical limitations and abilities, but they sure as fuck do not limit my ability to love myself, and it certainly does not define me. They do not dictate what we do with our lives – just maybe how we go about it. They are simply a vessel – an end to the means of what I can offer to this world, to myself, my kids, and my loved ones. The entire effing world.

We are constantly on a journey with our bodies. We are never done. We are becoming by constantly unbecoming and rebecoming. It's about the journey, right? There is no destination. With each experience, lesson learned, chosen perspective, and years added that give us wisdom – the journey will keep going.

My body is an extension of me, not the other way around.

And self-love, self-acceptance, and self-respect will reign victorious.

Every. Single. Time.

*Body bliss.*

IS NOT AN EITHER/OR THING. IT IS OKAY TO LOVE YOUR BODY AND STILL WANT TO CHANGE SOMETHING ABOUT IT.

# *A note*
# FROM THE PUBLISHER

Hey. You made it! I'm thrilled that you've picked up this book to support someone you know on their journey to becoming an author. There is massive power in women collaborating on big things, and I know I speak for every author in this book when I say… *Thank you.* Thank you for being here. For buying this book. Thank you for reading our stories, and holding space for us. Thank you for giving us your time and energy.

This is the first co-author book that I haven't contributed to since I began hosting group books in 2019. I started writing my own chapter, then the introduction, and then the foreword. And, the truth is, based on my history in business and my past as a body image and confidence coach, it would make total sense for me to write the foreword for this beautiful book.

BUT THIS ISN'T ABOUT ME.

It's about the authors who have courageously shared their hearts and souls with you through their writing. It's about YOU, the person holding this book, and your own journey to finding *body bliss*. It's about how unstoppable we can be, when we lift each other up.

I implore you to begin blazing your own path to body bliss, whatever that means to you. And, as so many of the women in this book have shared, **this path may not have an end point.** I've found that after working on my body image and self-esteem for many years, I have now come to land in a very balanced place, rooted in radical self-acceptance and personal accountability. In this place, I may not be in **love** with *every* part of my body all the time, but I have grown an immense respect for my body and all she has done (and continues to do) for me *every. Single. Day.* I have found peace in accepting that while my body is technically the "forward facing" piece of me that the world sees, you really cannot know how amazing I am (you know, if I do say so myself, haha!) unless you get to know me. The good stuff is INSIDE, not outside. And my body is just one (teeny, tiny, miniscule) percent of how awesome I am as a human being.

I KNOW THAT'S TRUE FOR YOU, TOO.

So, let go of what you have expected of your own personal image, and trust that you're in the body you're in for a reason, and she deserves to be loved and appreciated, no matter what size she is. You can love her and desire some change for her, but don't you dare despise her. That serves no one. Trust me on that.

YOU ARE WHO YOU ARE AND YOUR BODY IS THE WAY IT IS. WHATEVER. YOU STILL DESERVE TO SHOW UP, SPEAK UP, AND TAKE UP SPACE. OWN IT.

I hope you've enjoyed this book, because we have thoroughly enjoyed putting it together.

Writing a book is no small feat, and this masterpiece has taken months of hard work to bring to fruition. I am so proud of every single human being who has bared her soul inside these pages, and I encourage you to consider how you might do the same thing, even if it's just privately, for yourself, in a blank notebook. It's hella therapeutic.

If you haven't yet, be sure to connect with whomever you bought this book from, and tell them how much you loved their story. It will mean the world to them, I promise. More than money, or bestseller titles, or five star reviews… words have power. And your kindness will ripple for miles. (… Nautical miles. I just can't resist a good boat pun.)

Your own bliss will arrive in its own way, in its own time.

Trust the process and lean in, sister.

Thank you for being here.

***Courtney St Croix***
CEO, LeadHer Publishing

leadher
PUBLISHING

To find out more about LeadHer Publishing's books,
services, and collaborative projects,
visit leadherpublishing.com

Manufactured by Amazon.ca
Bolton, ON

26695475R00101